AGE

— OF —

INNOCENCE

THE CHILD PHOTOGRAPHY OF
CLIVE B HARRISON

FOREWORD BY
JORGE LEWINSKI

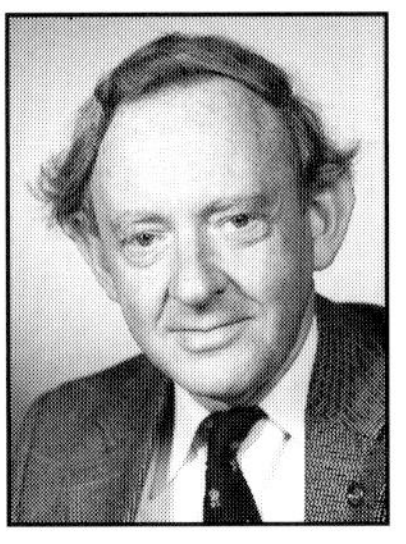

CLIVE HARRISON is a Fellow of the Royal Photographic Society and was a long serving member of its Licentiateship admissions panel. He is particularly noted for his candid photography of children, which has brought him many competition successes and exhibition awards. A member of the London Salon of Photography and the widely acclaimed Arena Group, his photographs have been seen in many prestigious exhibitions, magazines and books.

JORGE LEWINSKI, who provides the foreword, is a widely published professional photographer and photo-journalist. He has had several one-man exhibitions and his prints are included in the collections of, *inter alia*, the Victoria & Albert Museum and the National Portrait Gallery. His photographs have illustrated over 20 books.

AGE OF INNOCENCE
The child photography of
CLIVE B HARRISON FRPS

Published in the UK by Creative Monochrome
20 St Peters Road, Croydon, Surrey, CR0 1HD.

British Library Cataloguing-in-Publication Data:
A catalogue record for this book is available
from the British Library

ISBN 1 873319 14 2
First edition, 1994

Printed in England by The Bath Press,
Lower Bristol Road, Bath, Avon.

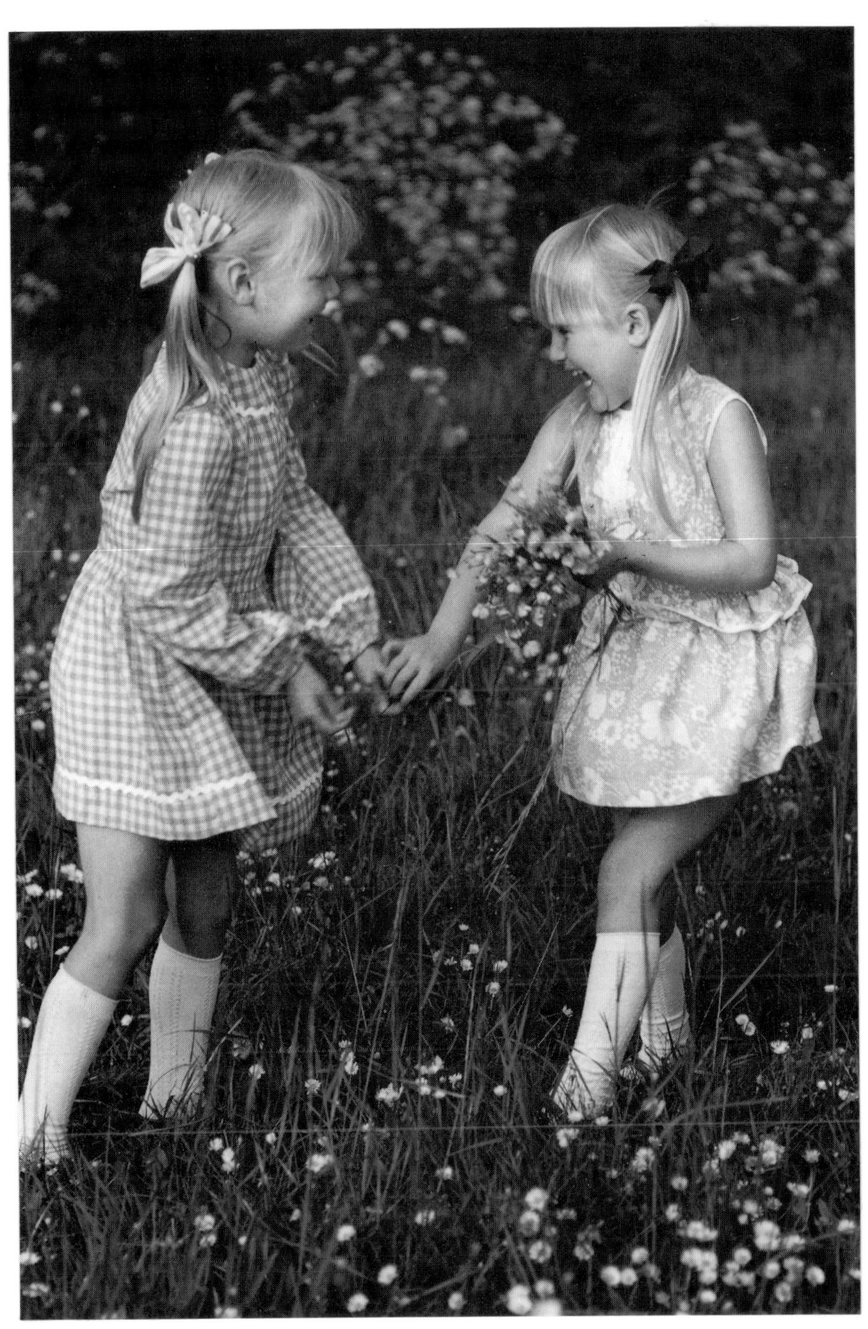

Foreword

Jorge Lewinski FRPS

Photography is an infinitely flexible medium of personal expression. It seems to me that in no other creative medium can the character and personality of an individual artist be so clearly discernible as in photography. Don McCullin's brooding, pessimistic nature; Bill Brandt's dark, gloomy and foreboding aspect of the world, and Doisneau's humorous and sunny disposition: all are distinctly seen in their best work. So too is Clive Harrison's character mirrored in his.

Clive is a gentle, modest and tranquil man – and so is his photography. In all the thirty or so years I have known him (we met in the 'fifties as novice amateur photographers at the Ealing Photographic Society), I have never heard Clive utter a single nasty word about anyone, nor have I seen any aspect of the cruel, malicious or ugly side of our world depicted in any of his photographs.

It is not surprising, therefore, that photographs of children (young children rather than teenagers) became his signature tune. It is also evident why Clive – a gentle photographer – has managed to develop such a close and intimate rapport with his subject. He likes children and it is evident that children like Clive.

But, of course, it is not as simple as all that. Clearly it is not enough to like your subject to be able to make good photographs. Most of the people flocking to the Lake District with their cameras adore the views – but very few produce great landscape images. What is required in addition to empathy with your subject is a great deal of skill and also deep sensitivity – the ability to respond emotionally to your subject and the skill to translate it into an image.

Many photographers maintain that children are possibly the most difficult subject for photography: far more difficult than a tranquil view of Windermere. Children are unpredictable, restless and often uncooperative. With children, a photographer requires infinite patience and a knack of 'snatching' what Cartier-Bresson called a 'decisive moment'. You also need a keen eye to be able to note, compose and press the shutter release just at the right moment, and often in a split of a second.

If a painter, for example, mainly relies on the synthesis of his emotions and impresssions, both actual and past, the photographer's forte is selection. Selection of a frame of what confronts his camera at just this precise moment. And what confronts it is rarely neatly and conveniently organised: reality is hardly ever orderly and uncluttered. Yet from this virtually random assembly of shapes, lines and various objects, a good photographer has to extract a pleasing and harmonious picture. A tall order indeed. And, let's face it, there are few more chaotic and uncontrolled subjects than a bunch of kids in full cry.

Leafing through the photographs on the following pages, one can plainly see that the photographer managed to overcome all these difficulties and has achieved his aim quite admirably. He has managed to retain, in all the pictures, the informality, immediacy and sheer joyfulness of childhood, while yet creating images of order and harmony.

It gives me a great pleasure to introduce to a wider audience the gentle art of Clive Harrison.

Introduction

Clive Harrison FRPS

To misquote an old song:

> *Other people's children, that's my line,*
> *Photographed dozens, none of them mine.*

So how did a bachelor and mechanical engineer come to be a photographer of children?

Trying to analyse it, I wonder if it was the inherited influence of my maternal grandfather, who was a keen amateur photographer long before my birth. It was he who took the first photographs of me, although looking through the family album, he does seem to have found the magnificent carriage-built pram, which was my early domain, rather more interesting than the tiny scrap inside. Sadly, he did not live long enough after my arrival to pass on to me personally the delights of his hobby.

The family album was continued by my parents with Box Brownie holiday snaps, supplemented by the occasional larger print from an itinerant beach photographer. One of these managed to depict me on the beach, sitting cross-legged, looking thin and toothless. This 'baby Gandhi' photograph, as it became known, remained – to my sustained embarrassment – a family joke for years.

At about four or five years of age, I fared better before the lens of the studio photographer at Frinton-on-Sea, a well known exponent of the daylight studio, trading under the name of Donovan. His warm tone, high-key portraits of me in my sailor suit, with a tint of blue added to my eyes and the merest hint of pink to my cheeks, made me look positively angelic. Unfortunately they were not judged to be good enough to be included in his subsequently published book, which I eventually bought many years on.

The family album was interrupted by the war and resumes with a photograph of me at about 13 in my new Scout uniform. This further source of embarrassment seems to have prompted me to take control of the family camera – thereafter only photos of my parents and friends appear in the album. I do not reappear until a group photo at Technical School.

It was around this time, about the age of 16, when I got the photographic bug and felt the need for a 'real' camera. This would have been around the end of 1949. I remember my father taking me into the camera shop near the London bank where he worked. When I described the photos I wished to take, it was recommended that I should buy a 'reflex' camera. I came away with a second-hand "two-and-a-quarter square" twin-lens Ikoflex. I thus declared myself a serious photographer and sometime later joined Wimbledon Photographic Society.

The most readily available subjects were those around me every day: namely the children of my parents' friends, most of whom had married during or just after the war. Thus, at the beginning of the 1950s, their personal boom of children was five to eight years old. Thus started my snapping of "other people's children".

A few years later, my college engineering training completed, I started work and was able to afford a new MPP Microcord TLR and, for colour slides, a Voigtlander Vito B 35mm camera. By this time, the family had moved to Ealing, where I joined the photographic society and met another new – somewhat more advanced – member, Jorge Lewinski. It was he who introduced me to the evening classes at the Ealing 'Tech' department of photography, where 'Walter' Marynowicz was soon trying to instil in us the principles of portrait lighting, providing glamorous young ladies and 'colourful' old gents for us to practice on.

Towards the end of the fifties, I discovered foreign travel where, especially in the Mediterranean area, there were always many children playing in the streets. These kids were usually keen to pose for a tourist's camera, but I preferred to catch them unawares and thus get more candid images.

In 1967, I followed my employers to Bracknell in Berkshire, where I bought a house on a new estate. I was the third person to move into what was still a building site. As the houses were completed and occupied, more and more children played amongst the sand and the mud. By the next summer, with the sand having been used for its intended purpose and the mud covered by grass, I had been adopted by some as a useful 'uncle' to be dragged off to fetes, fairs and sports days. Thus, a new generation of children came before my cameras, which by this time comprised a Rolleiflex F and a Retina Reflex S.

As local events palled, London was discovered with its much wider range of events. When the children of my friends and neighbours grew out of being taken to such events, I kept going, continuing to focus my cameras on children during their age of innocence. Why? Is it because they are easier to photograph than adults? Despite what many people say, I think this is possibly so: once children have satisfied their initial curiosity about a cameraman, they usually quickly return their attention completely to their tasks or re-enter their own fantasy worlds, while adults tend to remain more aware and self-conscious. Perhaps because children are themselves less inhibited and so imaginative, they present a livelier and more varied image than their grown-up counterparts.

I do, of course, photograph many other subjects, because photography has become a way of life. It sustained me while I was working as an engineer and has continued to do so since early retirement. The cameras have changed – I now use 35mm for monochrome as well as colour slides – but otherwise life goes on in much the same way. Last night, for example, I grabbed my camera as boys from the other end of the street came to do battle with the young girls from next door: the 'war' raging across my front path.

Although I photograph more adults nowadays, it is children during their age of innocence who usually present me with my best shots. Bless them! My sincere thanks to every one of them I have snapped over the years, and especially those who appear in this book. I hope the images will give you, the reader, as much pleasure in the viewing as they gave me in the making.

Portfolio

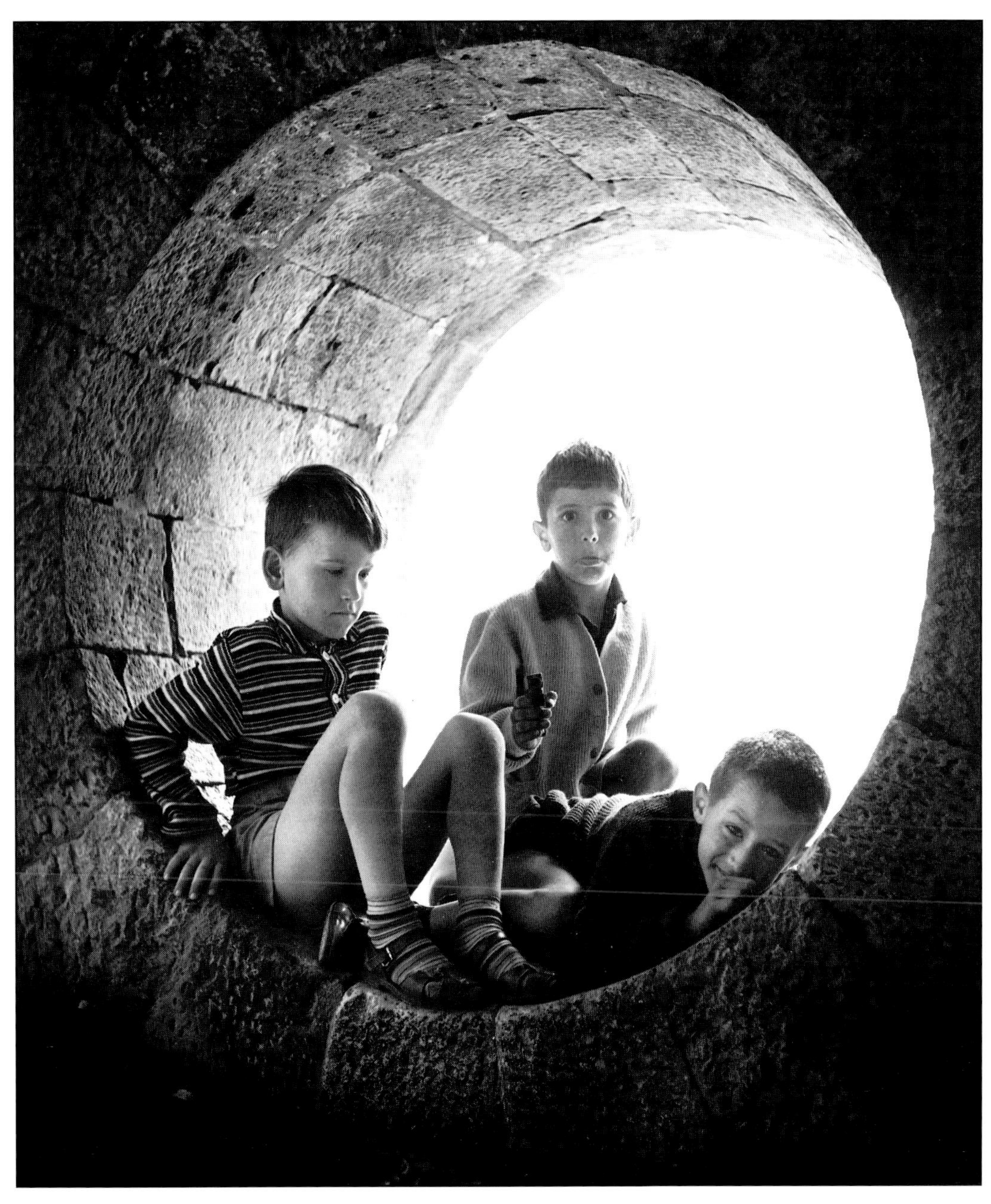

The hole in the wall
Dubrovnic, Yugoslavia, 1964

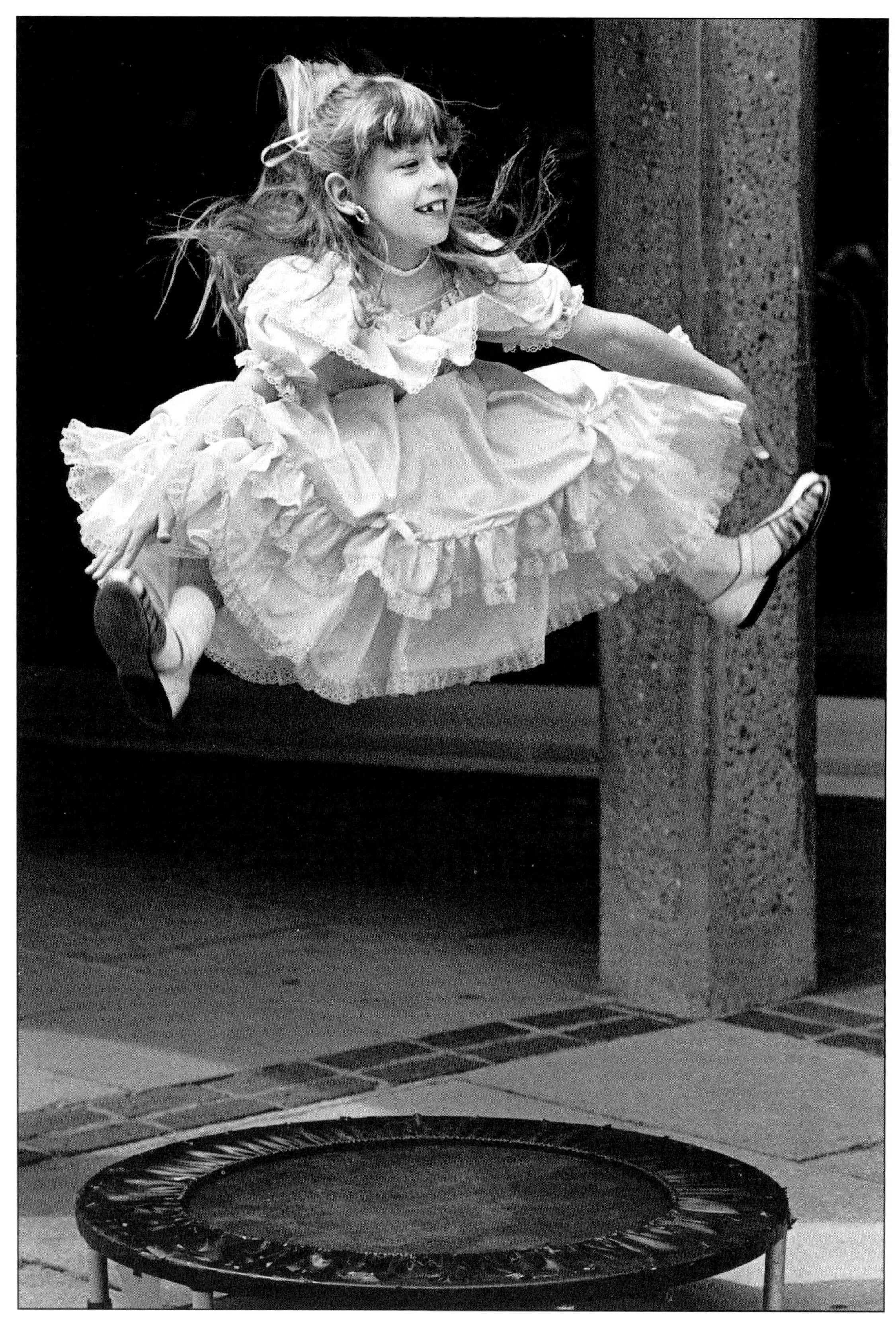

Bouncing girl
Dickens festival, Rochester, Kent

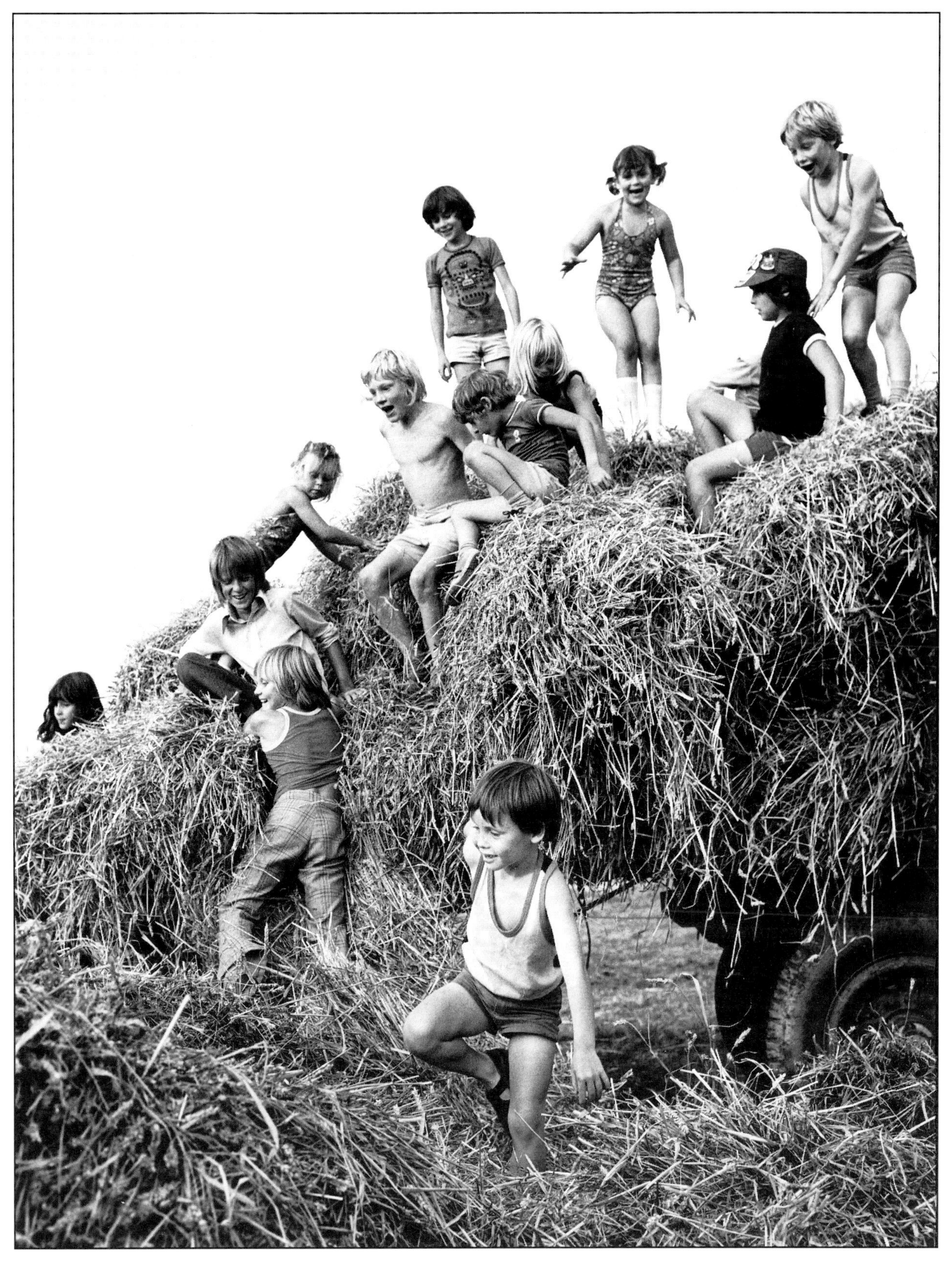

Haytime fun
Knowl Hill steam fair, near Reading, Berkshire

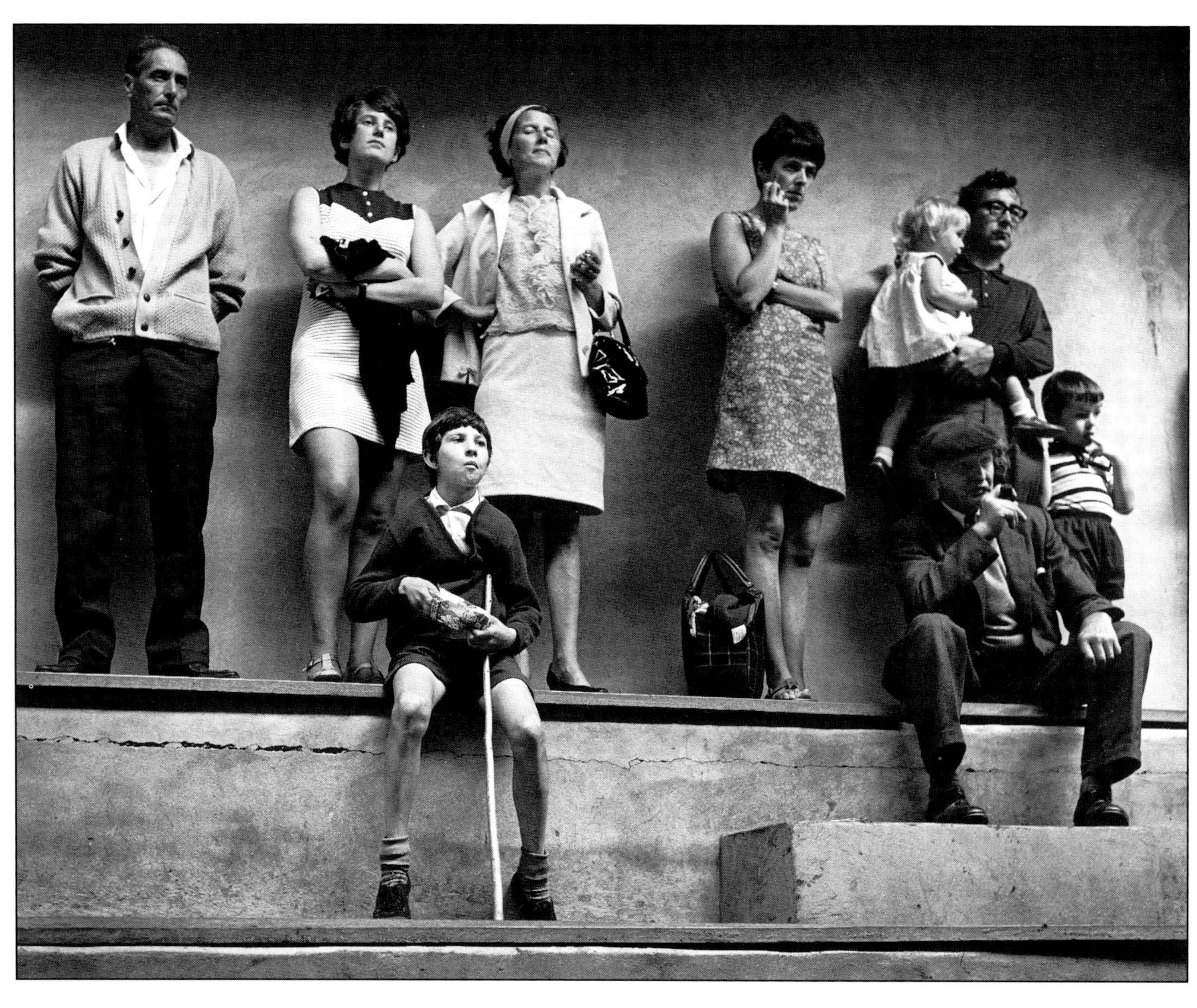

Boy in the audience
Cattle auction, Carmarthen, Wales

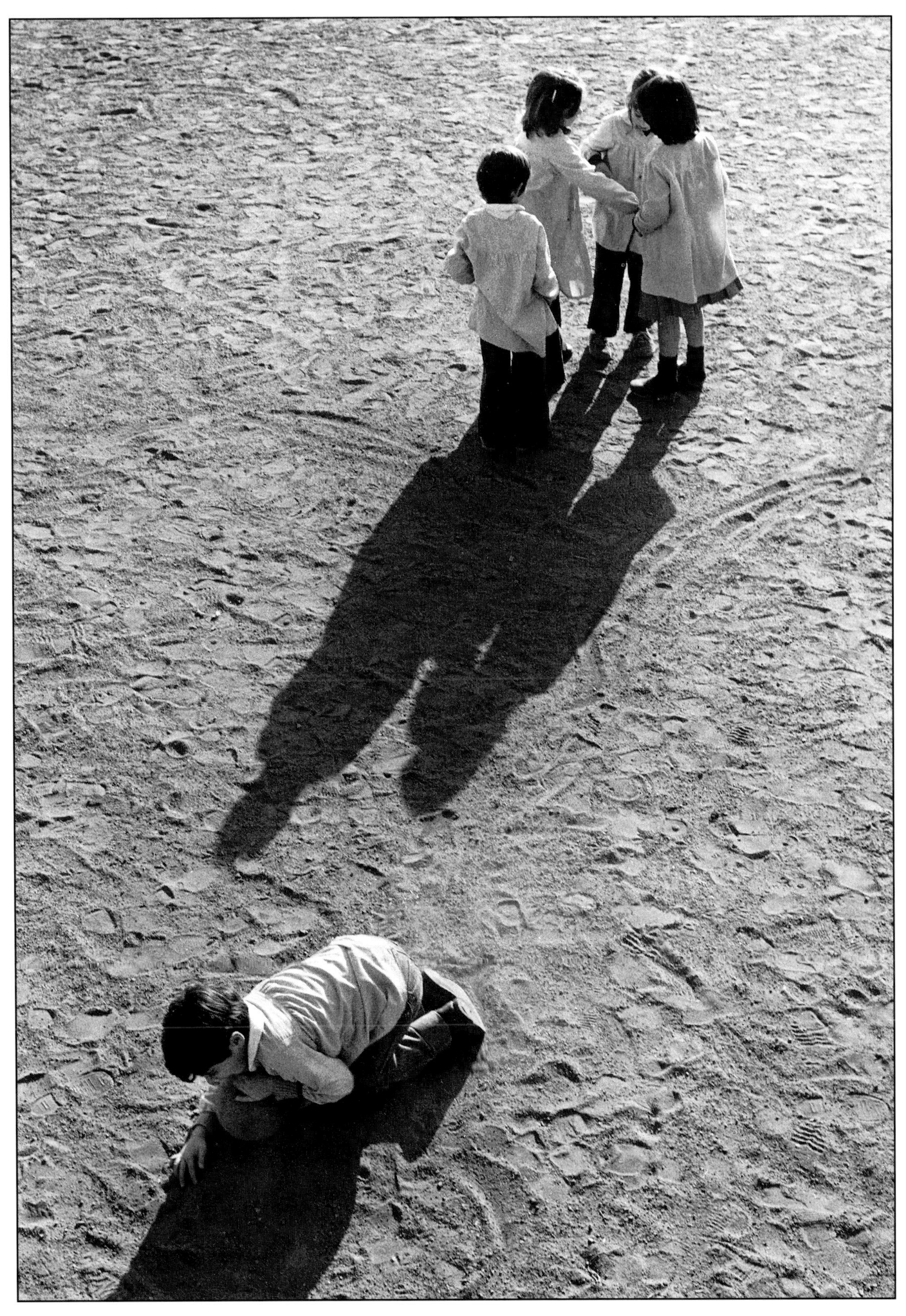

Hogging the ball
Barcelona, Spain

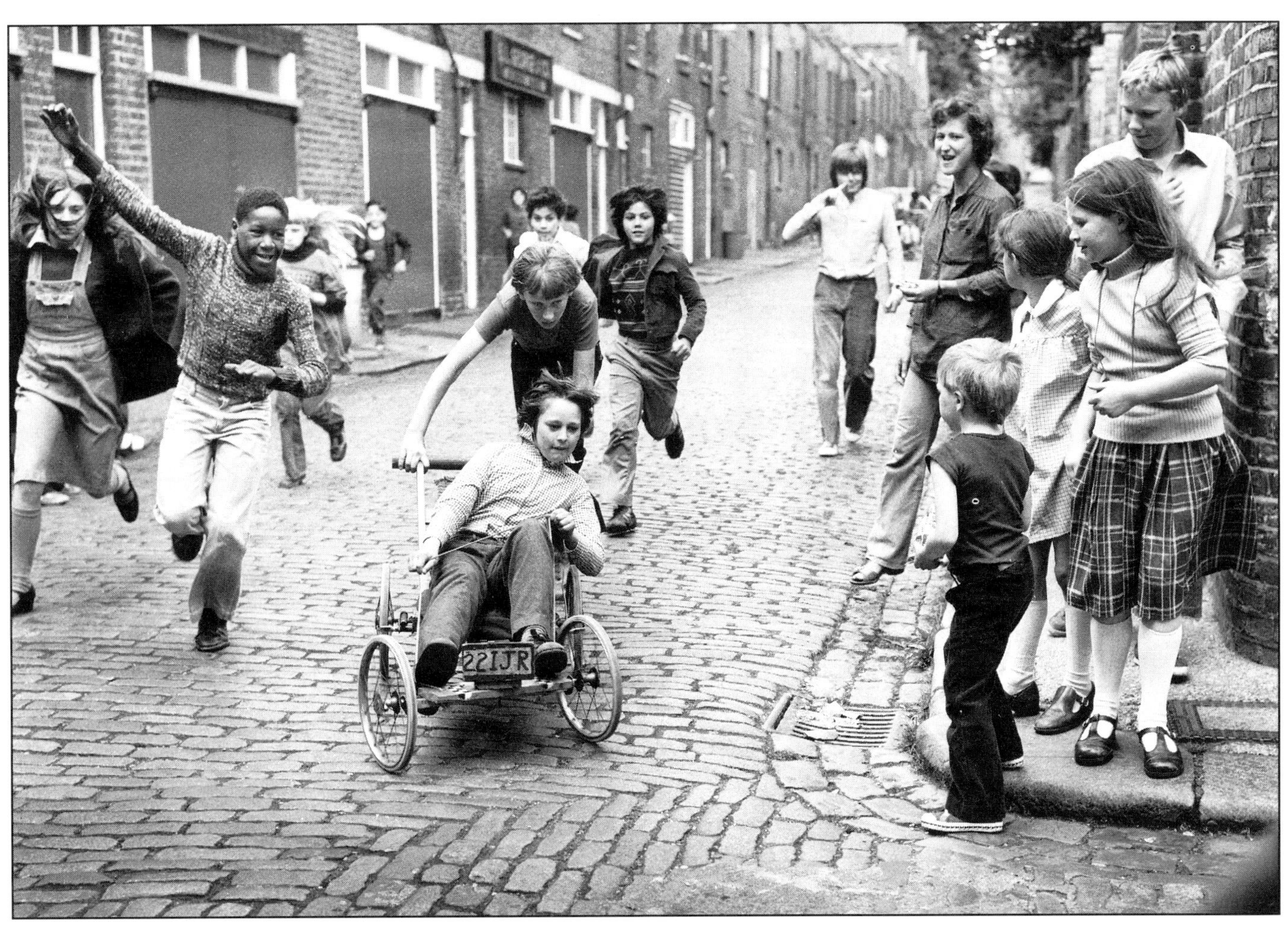

Going round the bend
Camden Community Festival, London

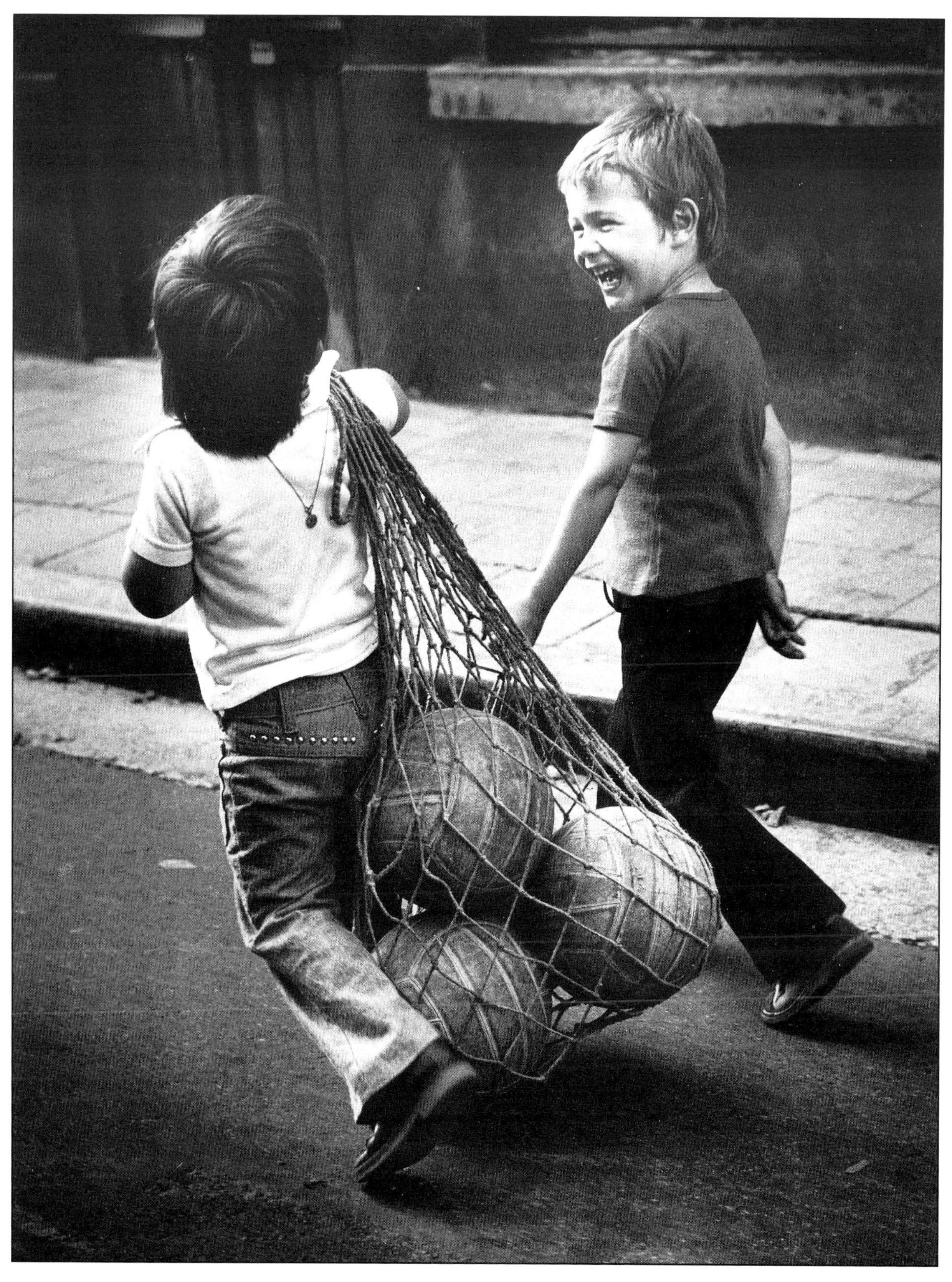

Ball boys
Street party, Brugges, Belgium

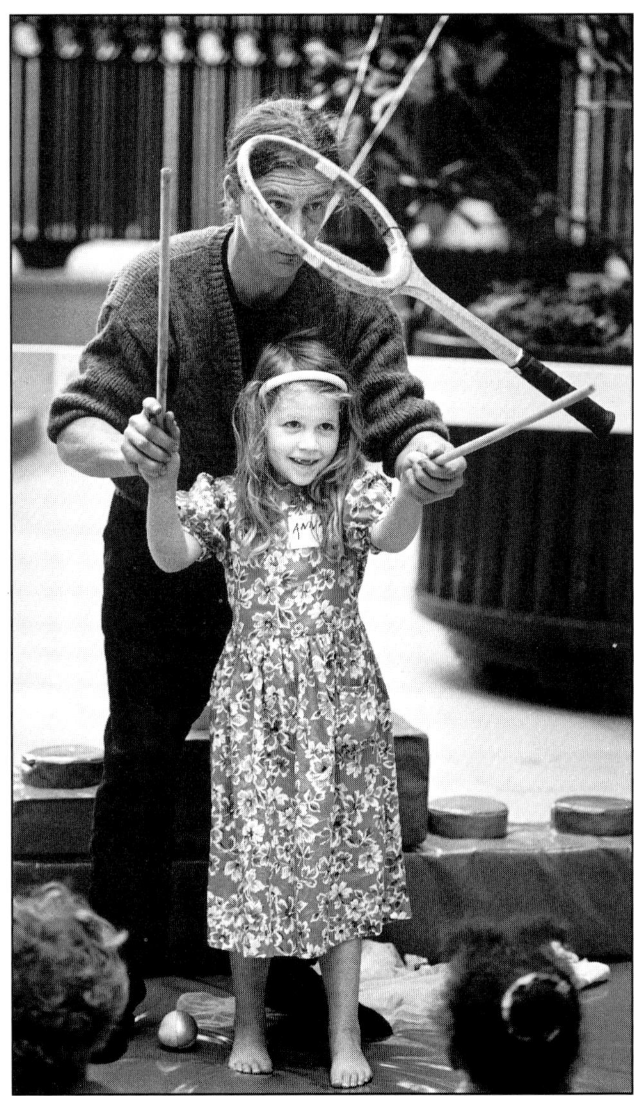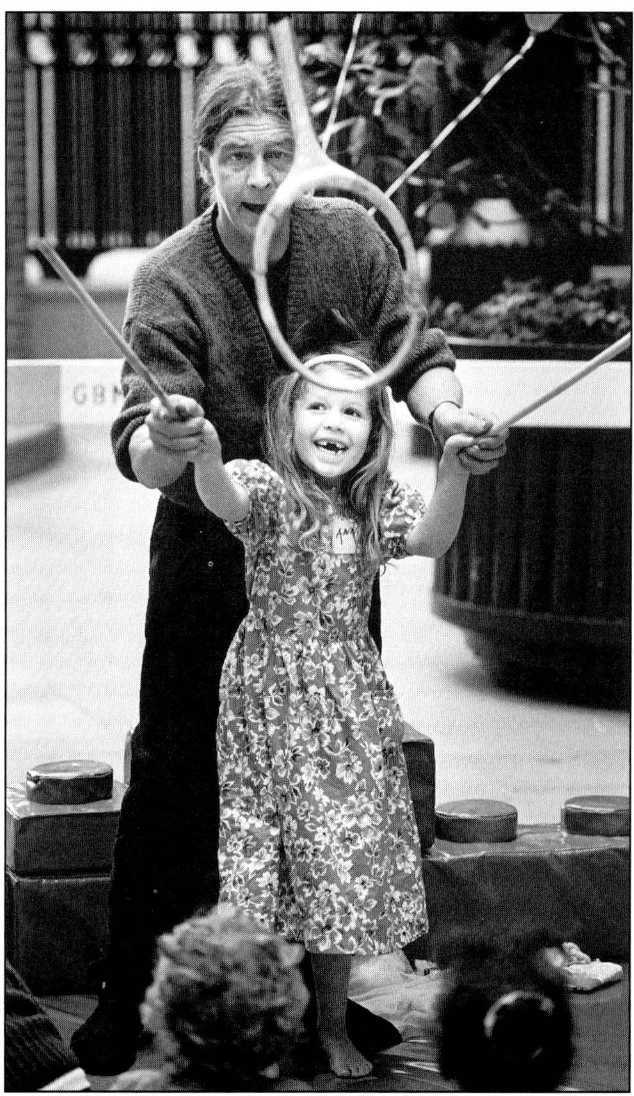

Anna discovers juggling
Hay's Galleria, London

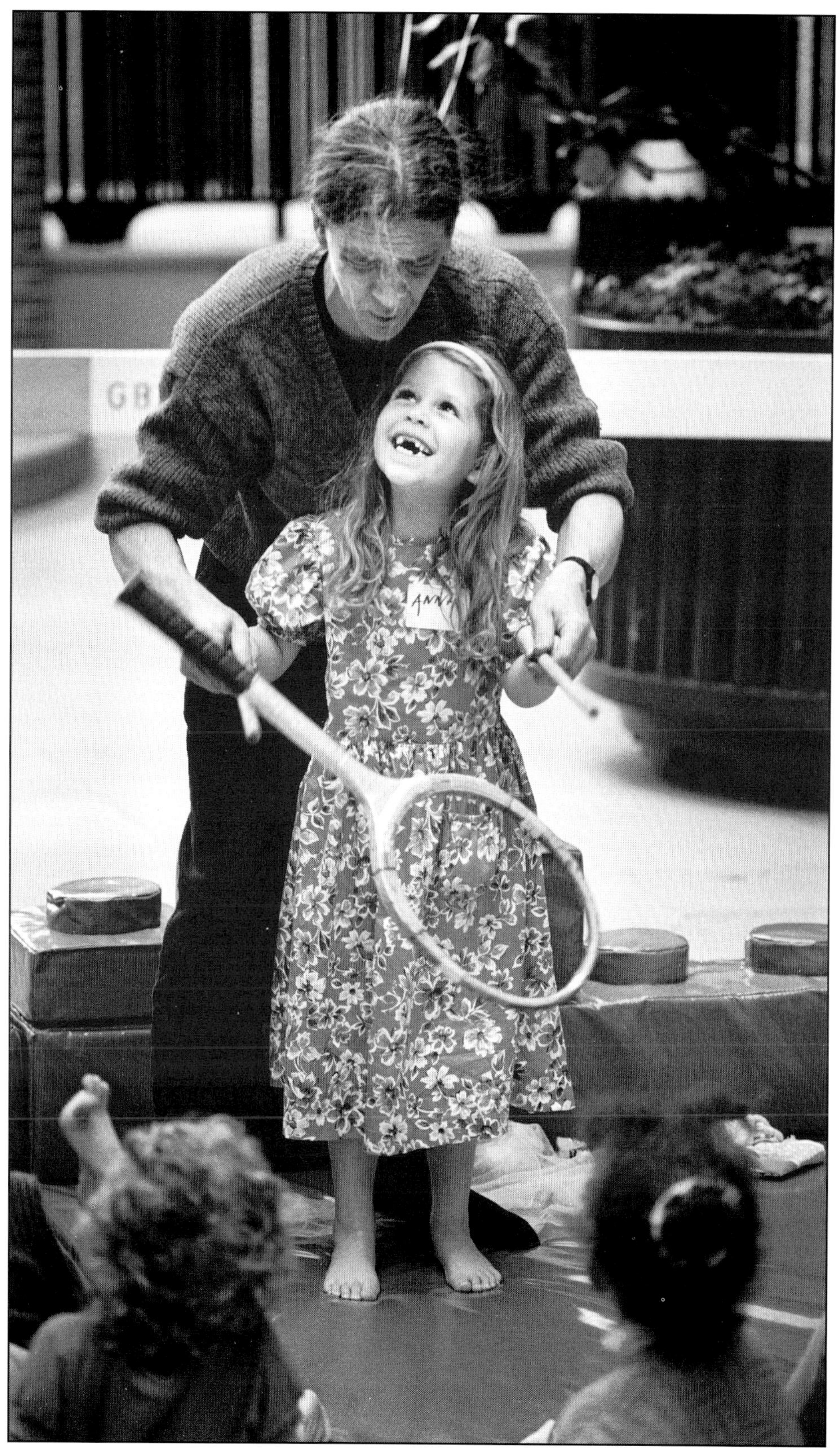

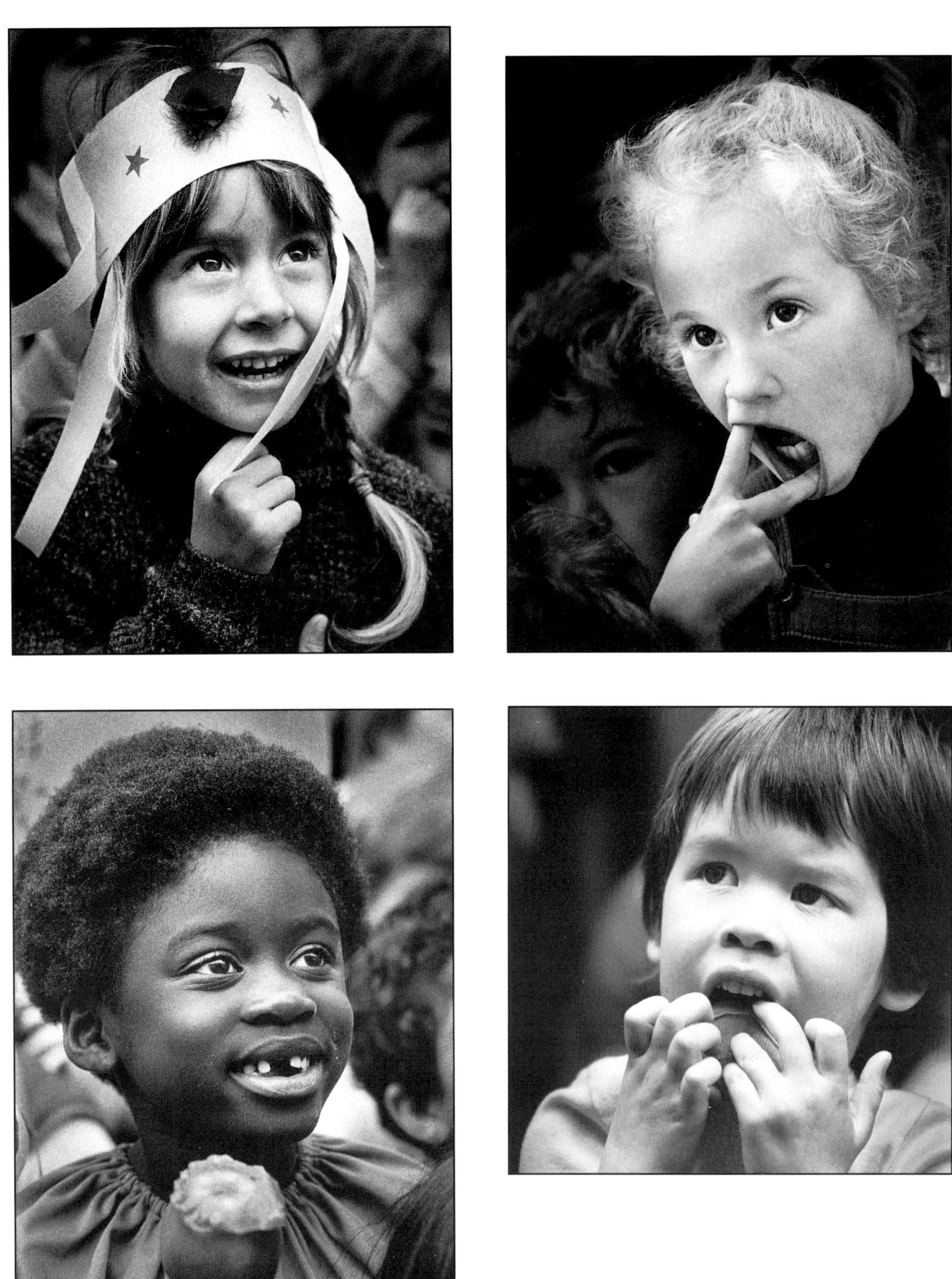

Reactions to Punch and Judy shows
London and Richmond, Surrey

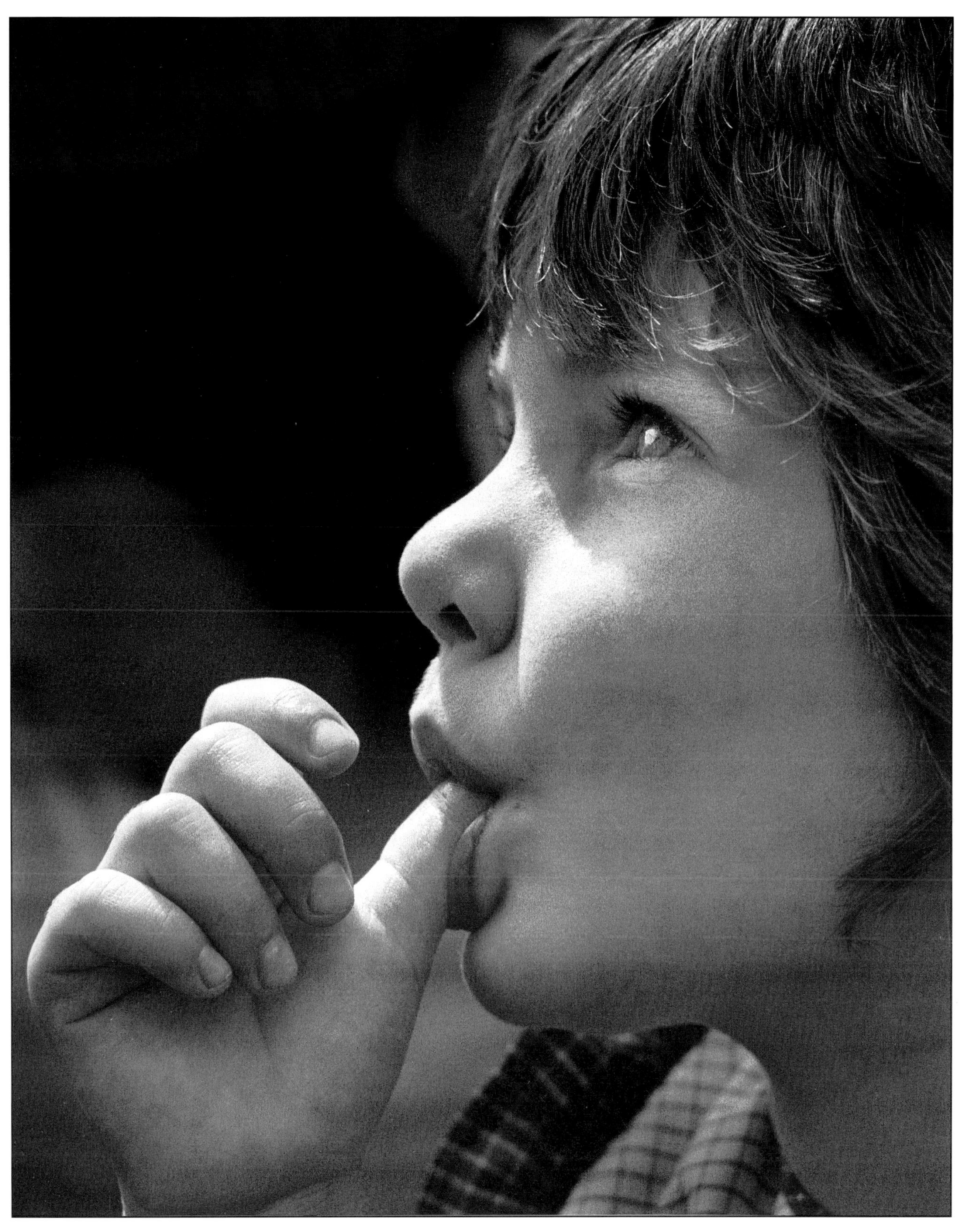

Concentration
Punch and Judy show, Spring Fair, Richmond, Surrey

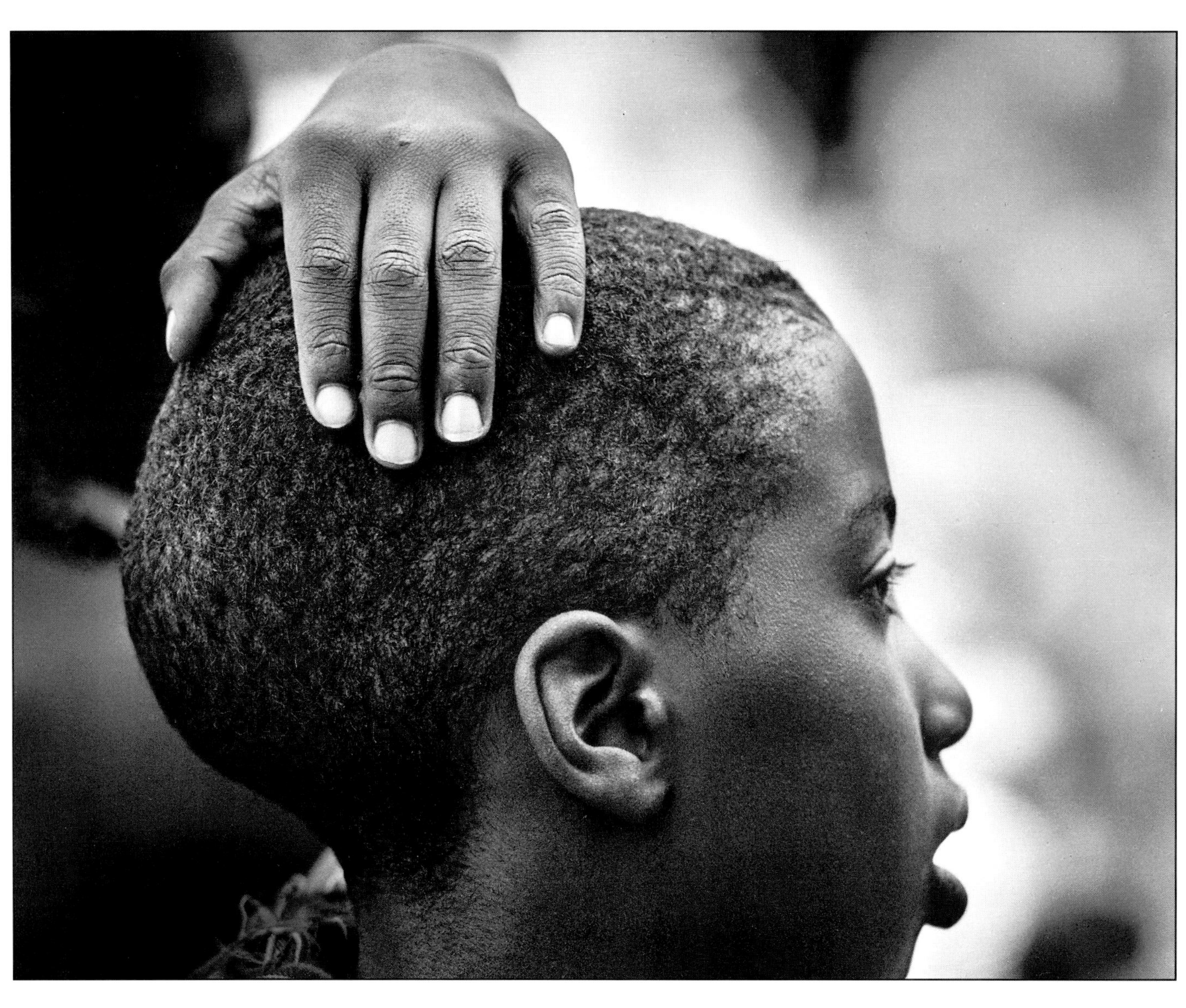

Head boy
Children's event, Covent Garden area, London

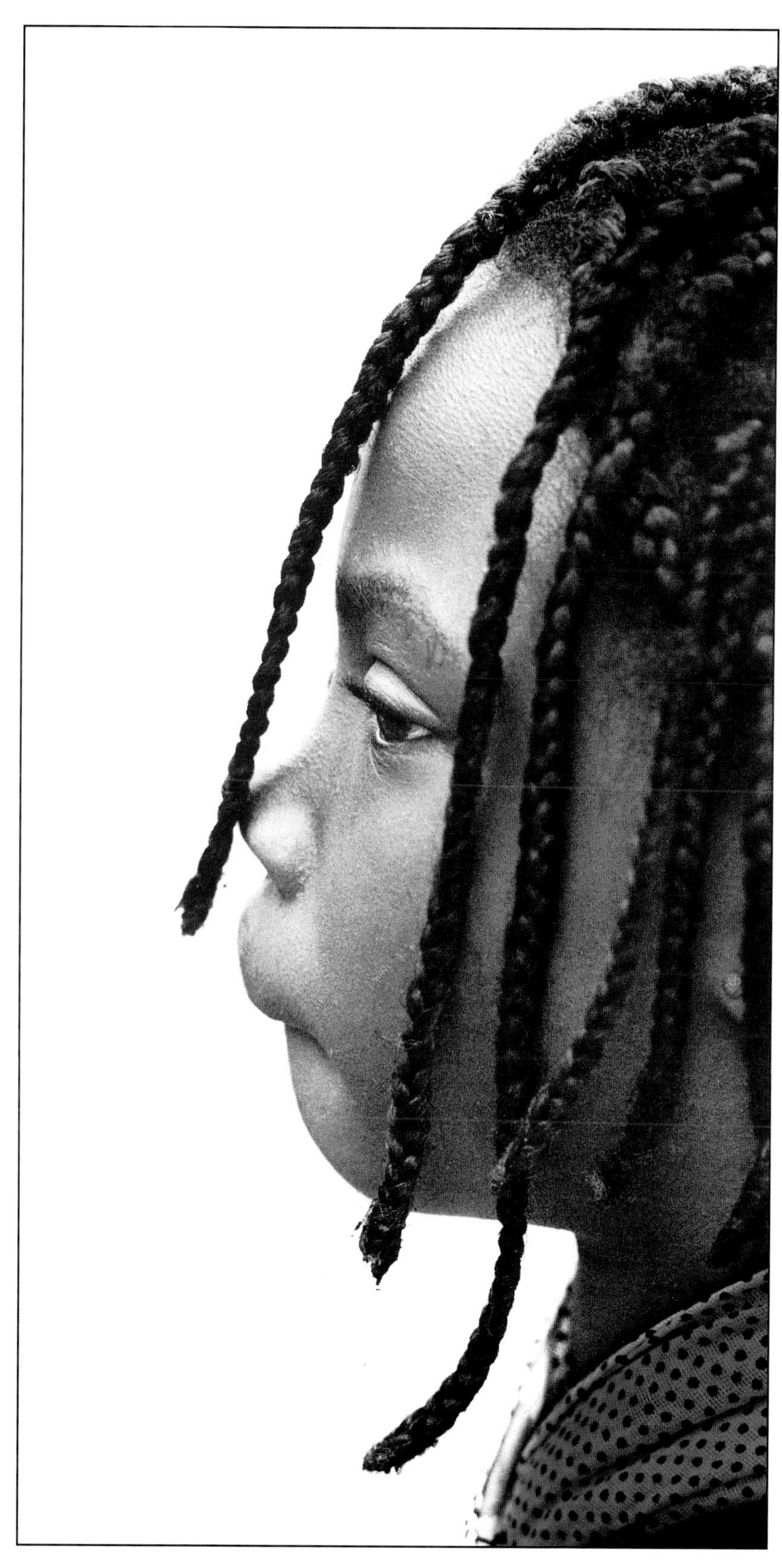

Pensive child
Children's event, Covent Garden area, London

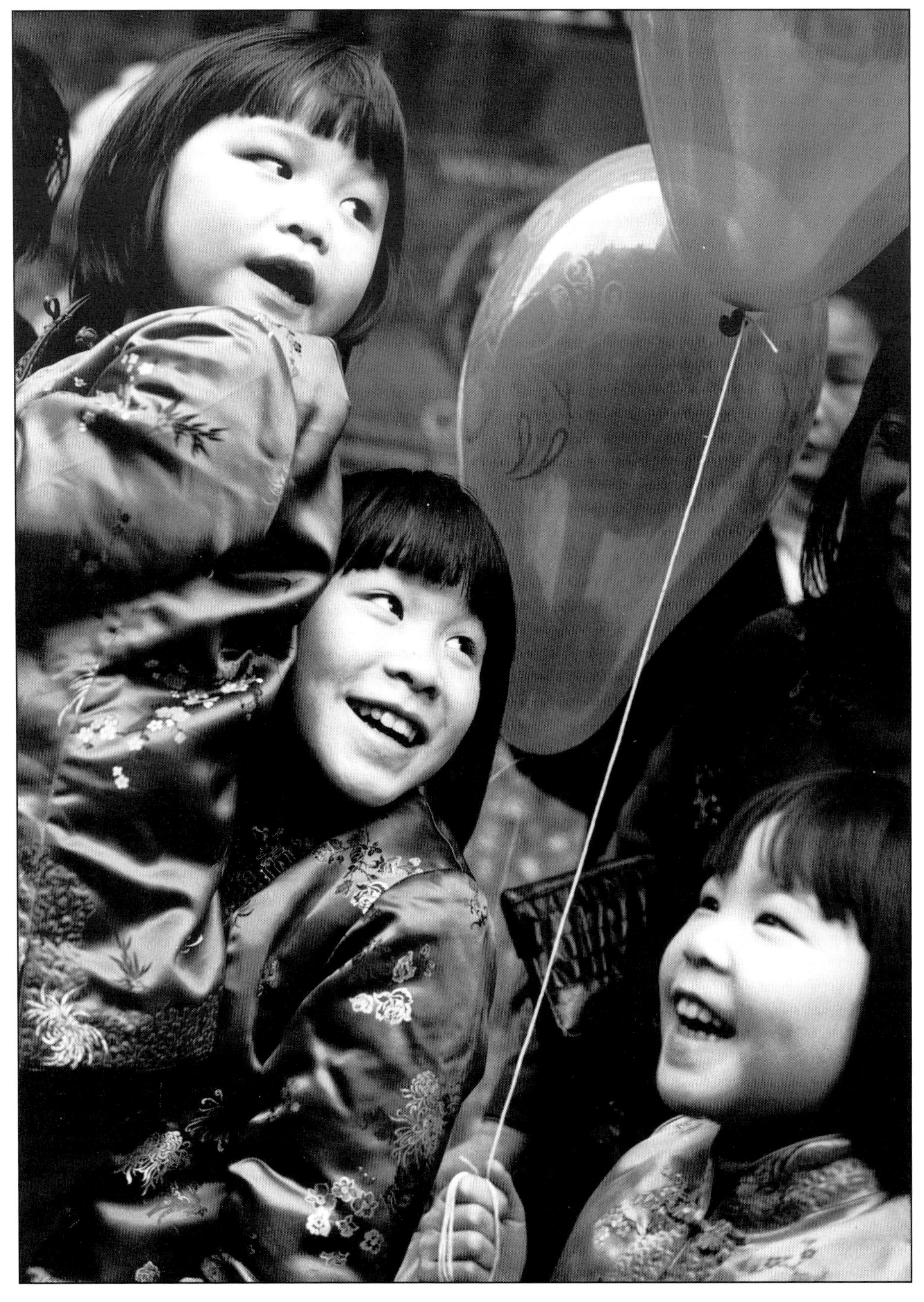

New Year Faces
Chinese New Year celebrations, London

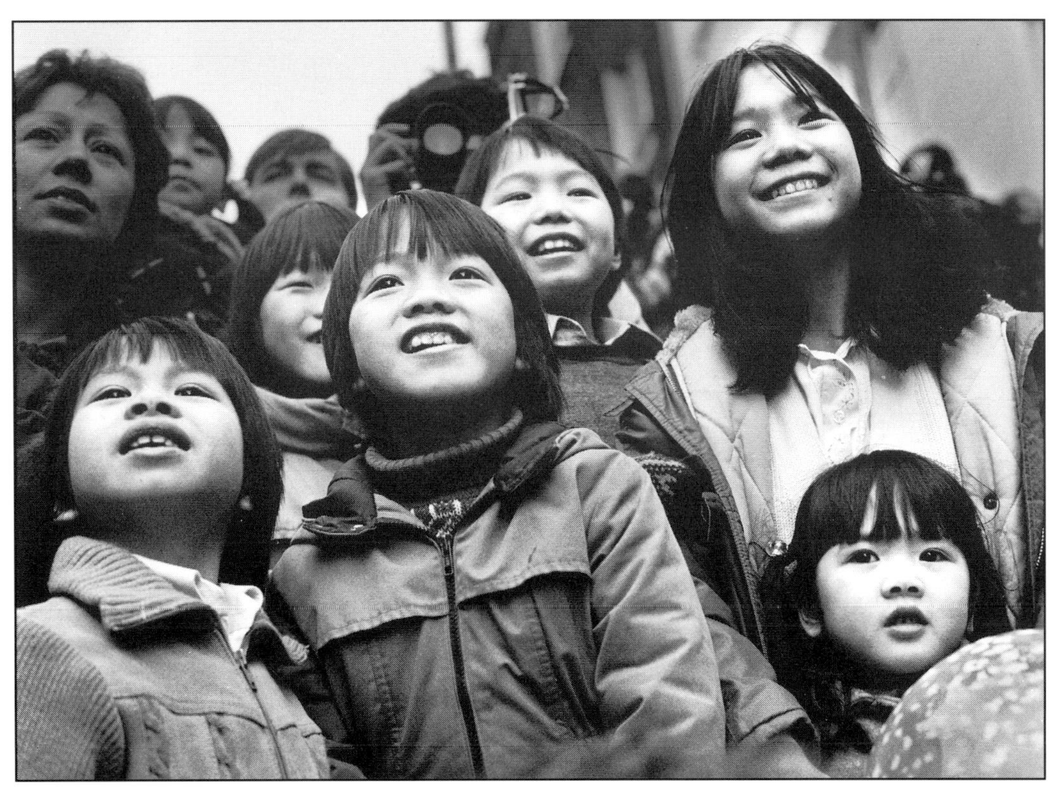

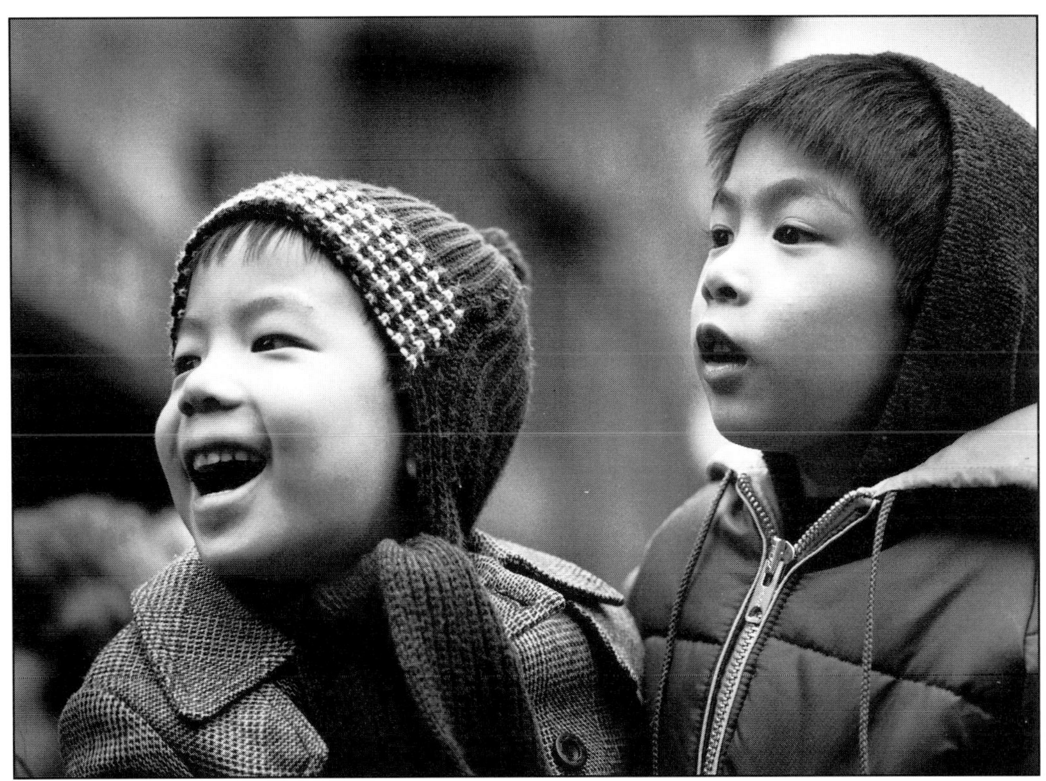

Catching sight of the dragon
Chinese New Year celebrations, London

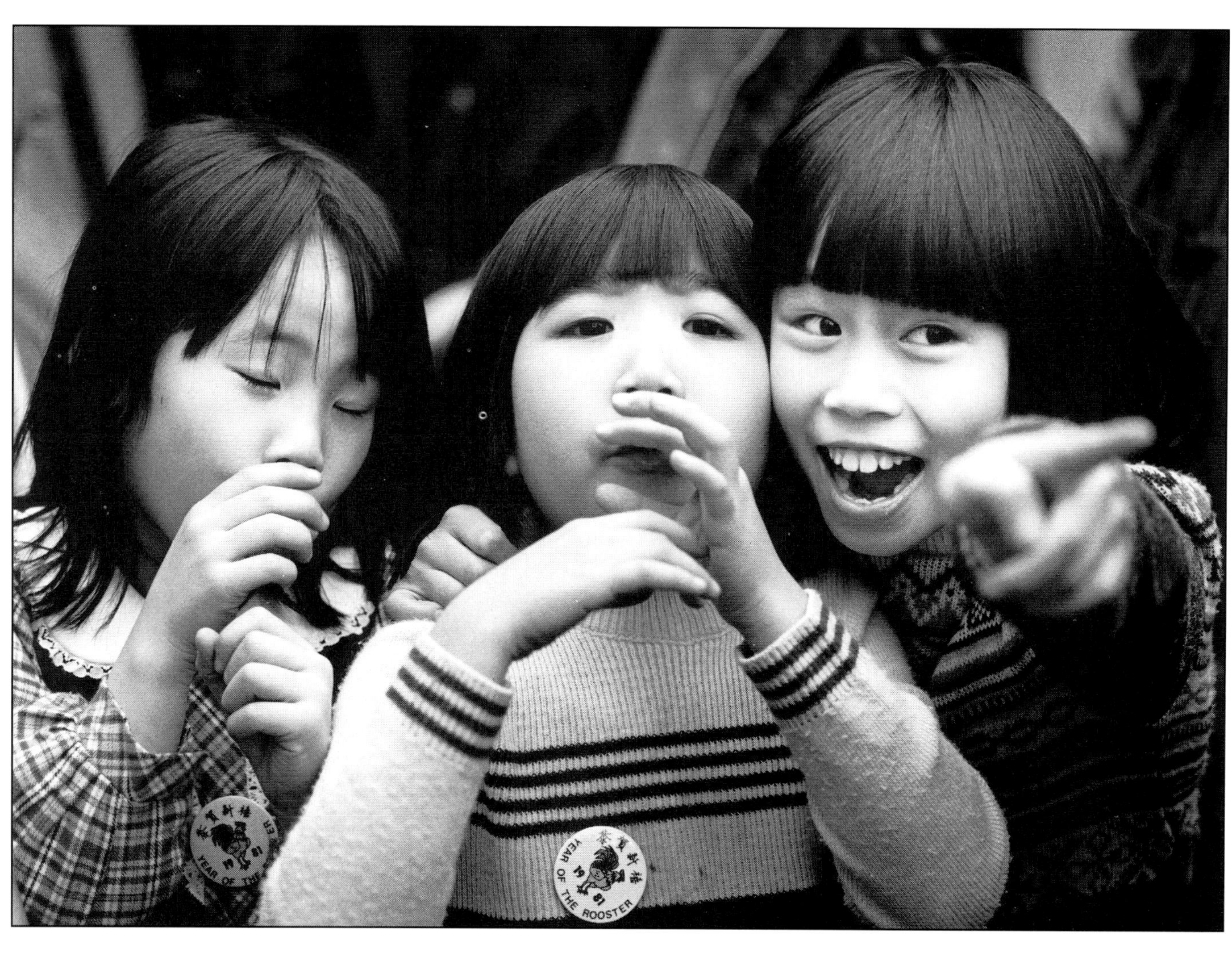

Copying the musicians
Chinese New Year festival, London

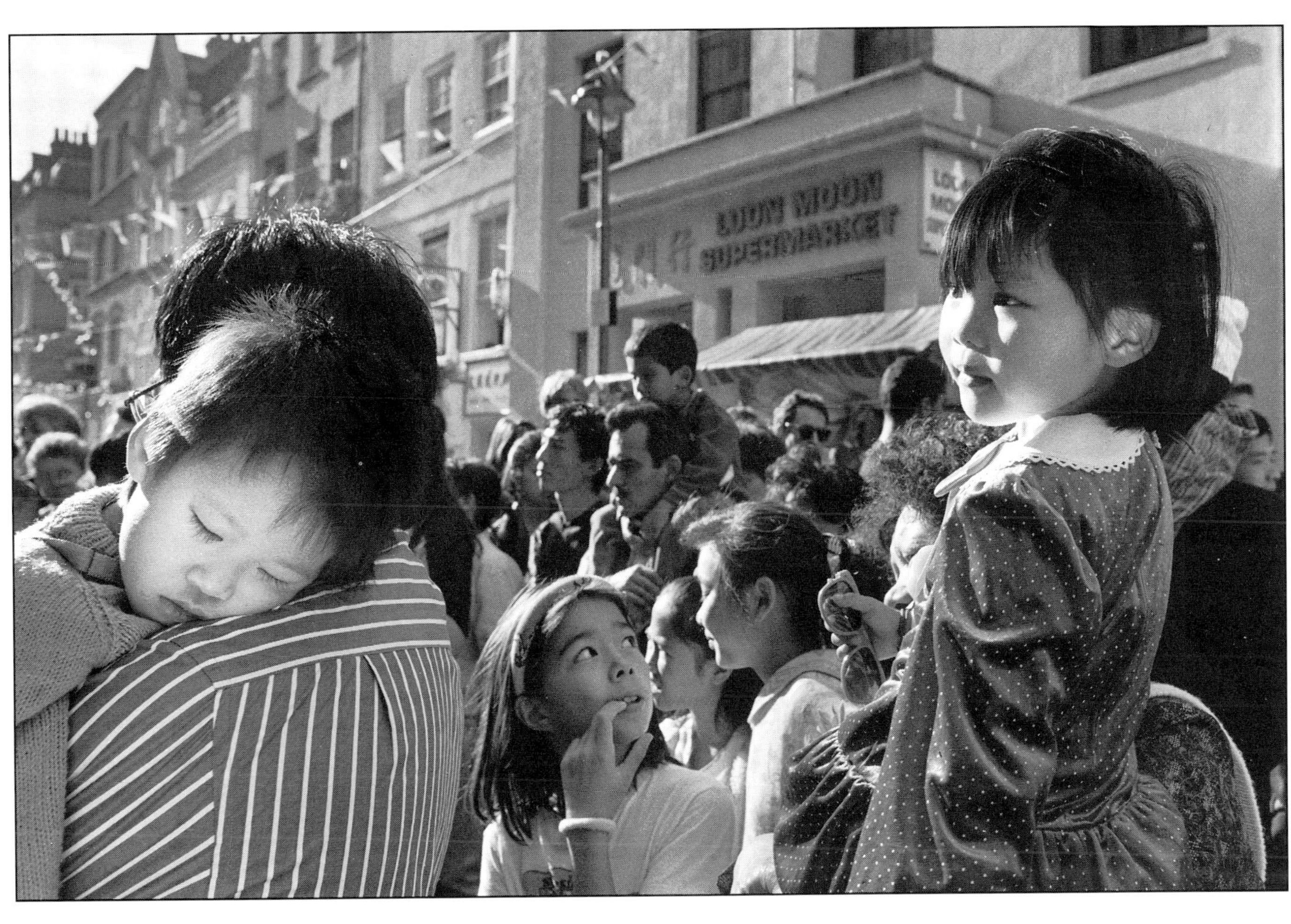

Missing the dragon
Chinese mid-Autumn festival, London

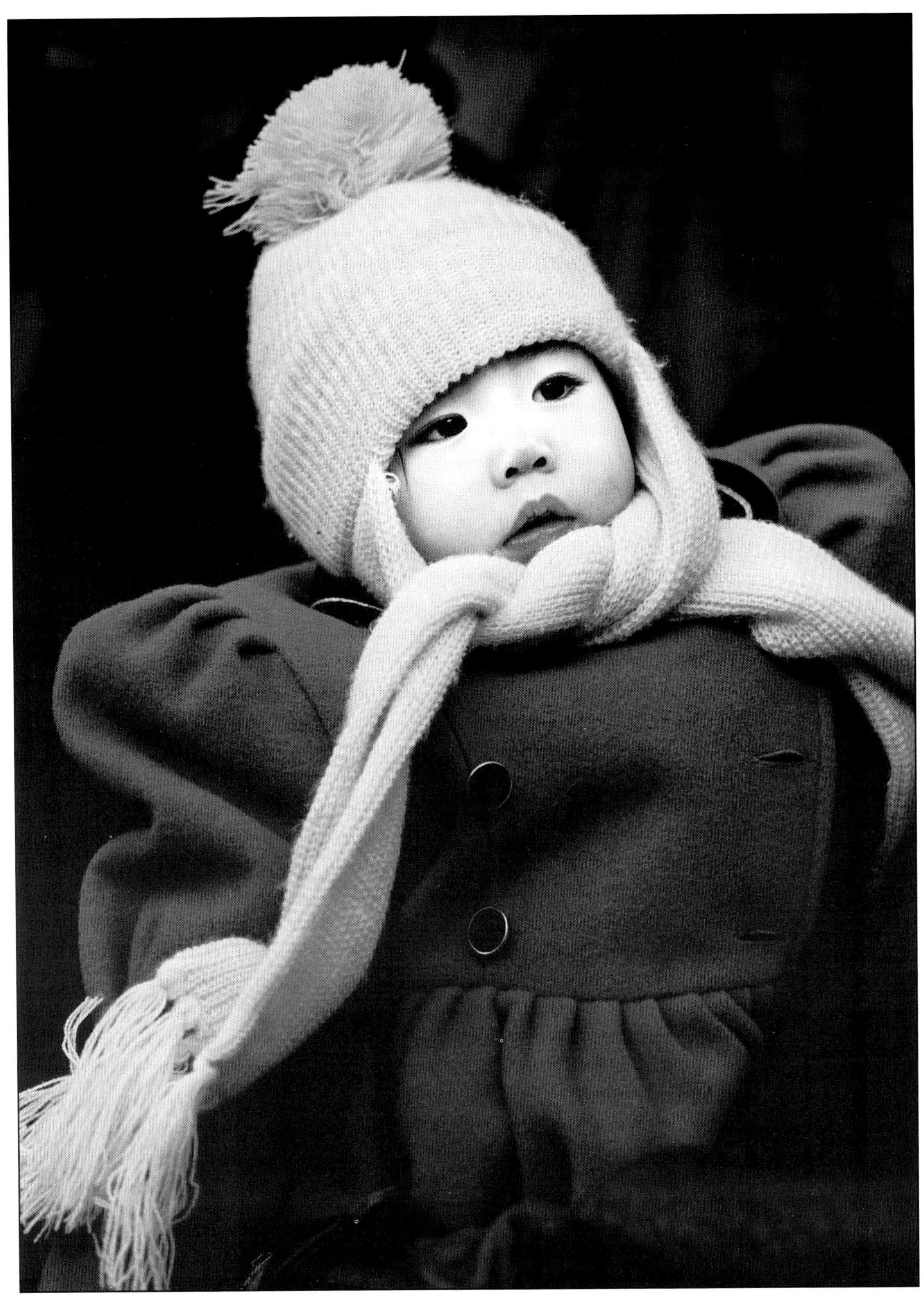

Warm for New Year
Chinese New Year festival, London

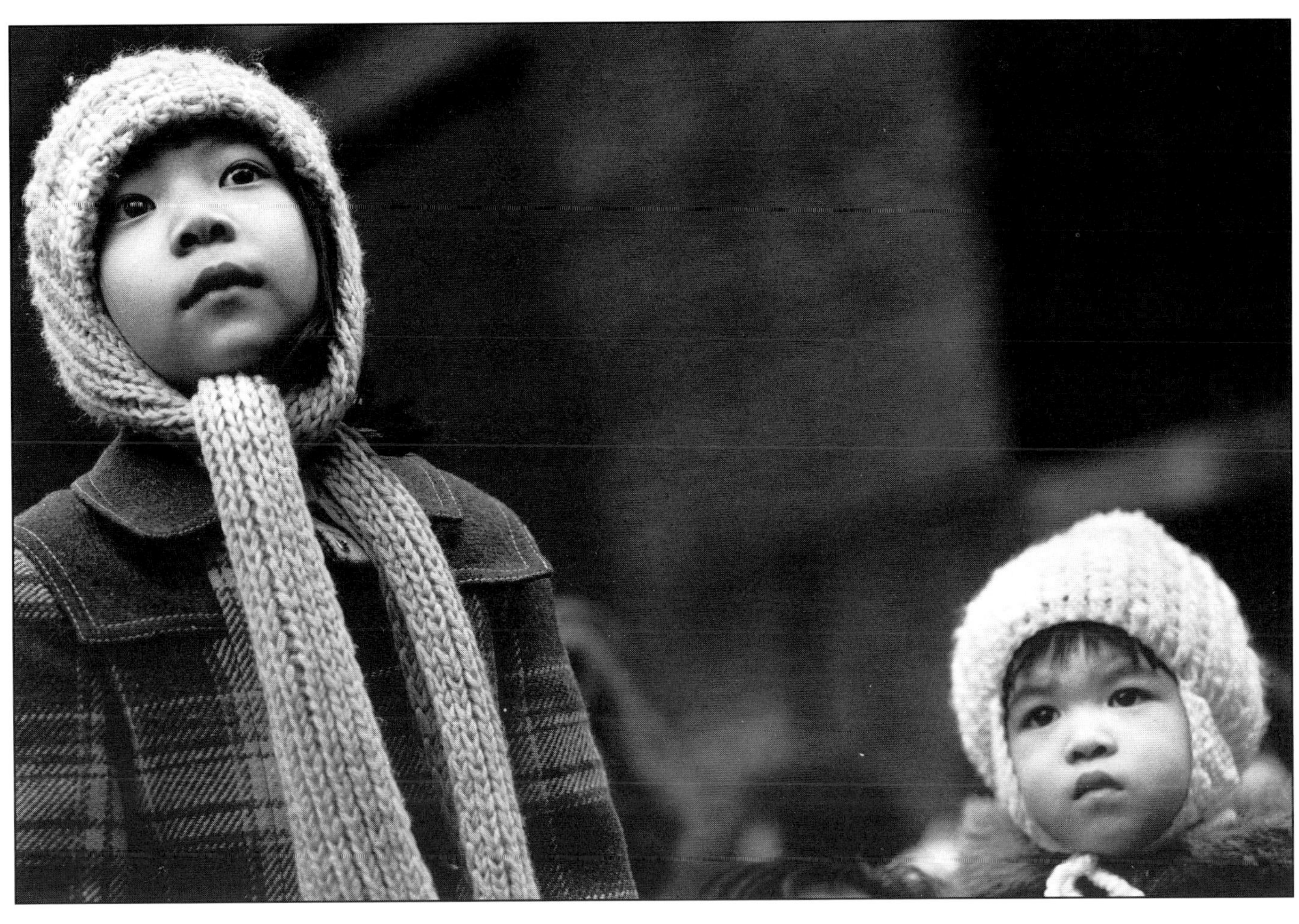

Waiting for the dragon
Chinese New Year, London

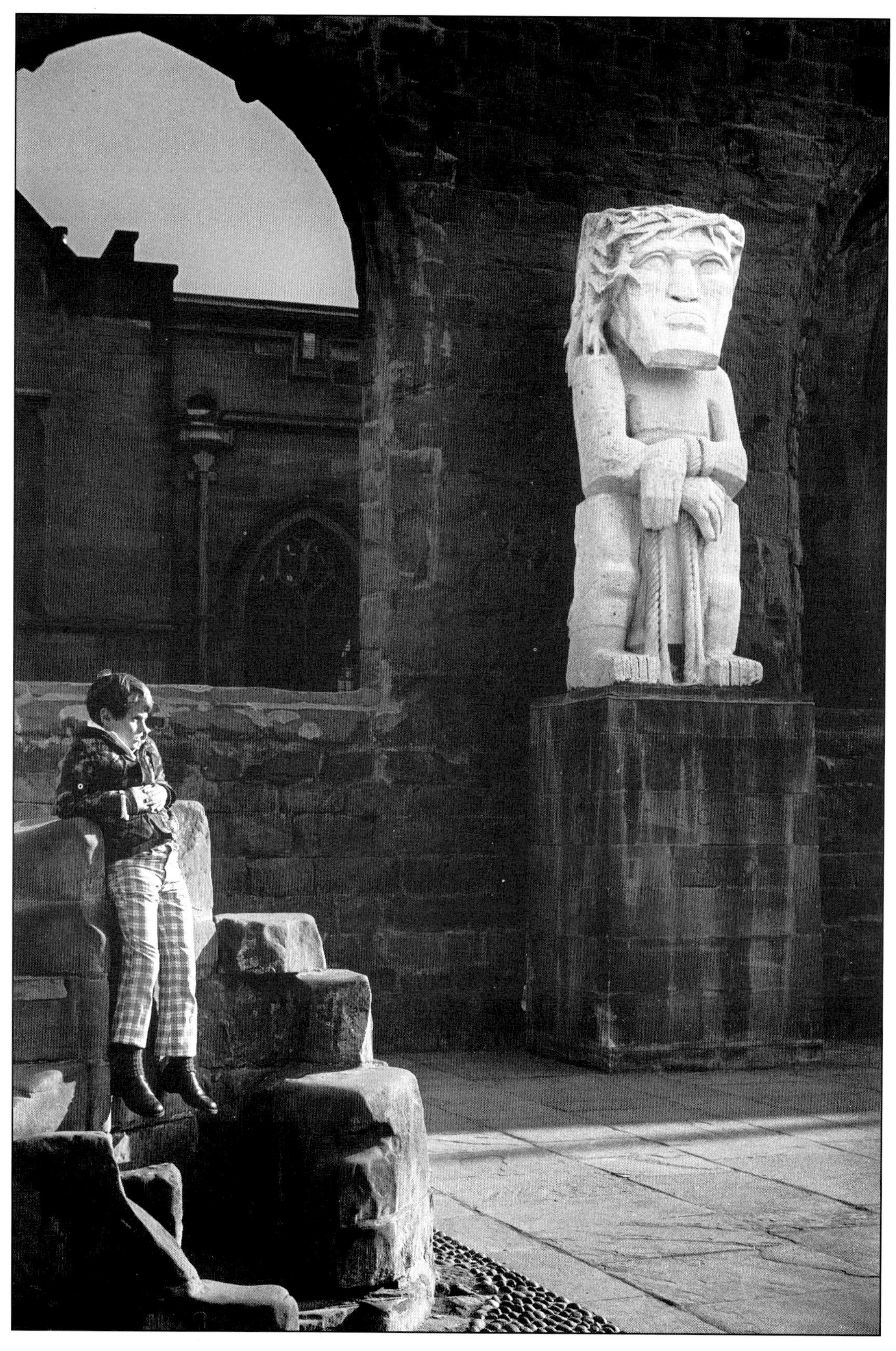

Epstein echo
Coventry

Childlike, I danced in a dream;
Blessings emblazoned that day;
Everything glowed with a gleam;
Yet we were looking away!

from The Self-Unseeing,
Thomas Hardy

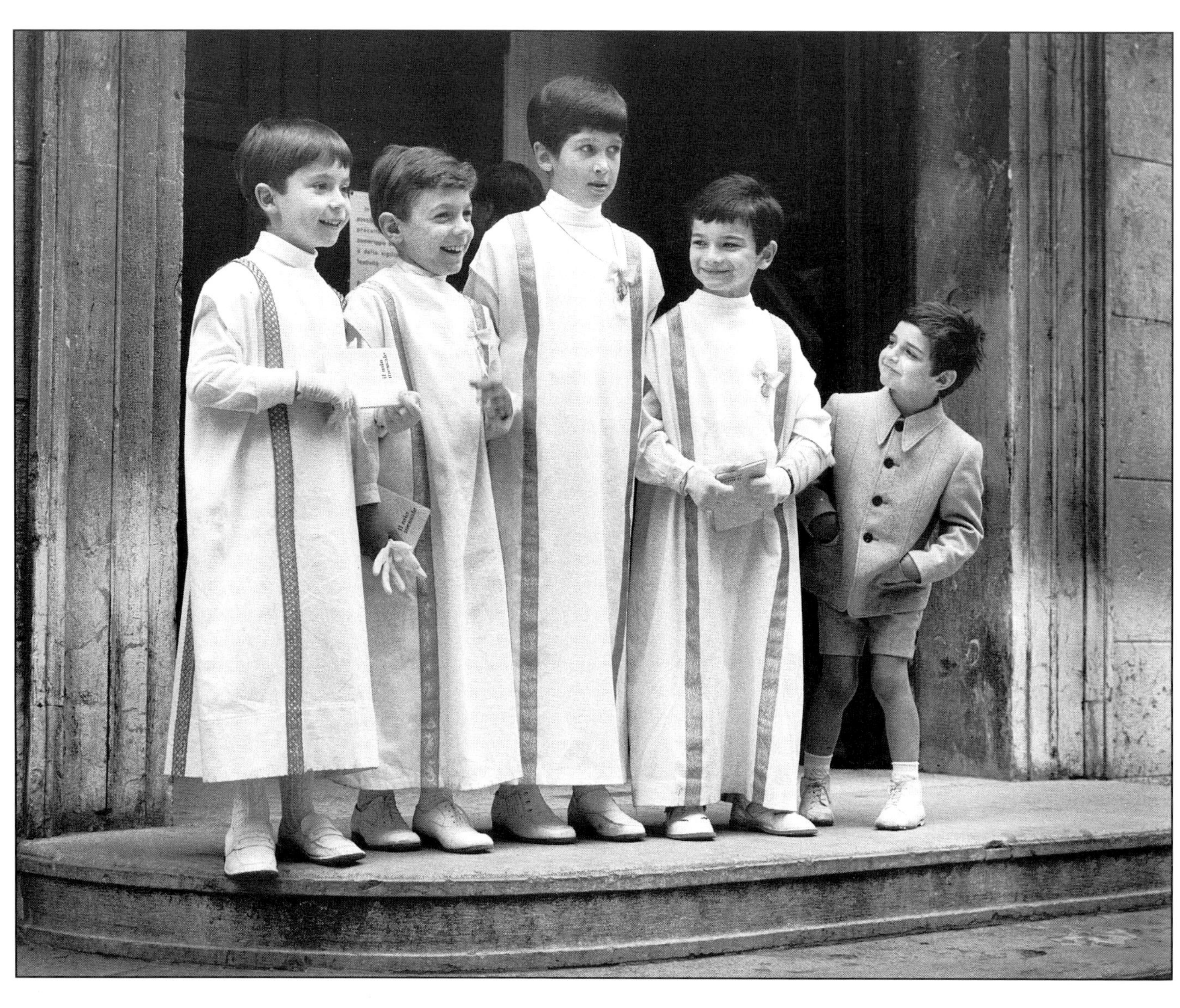

First Communion group (plus little brother)
Venice, Italy

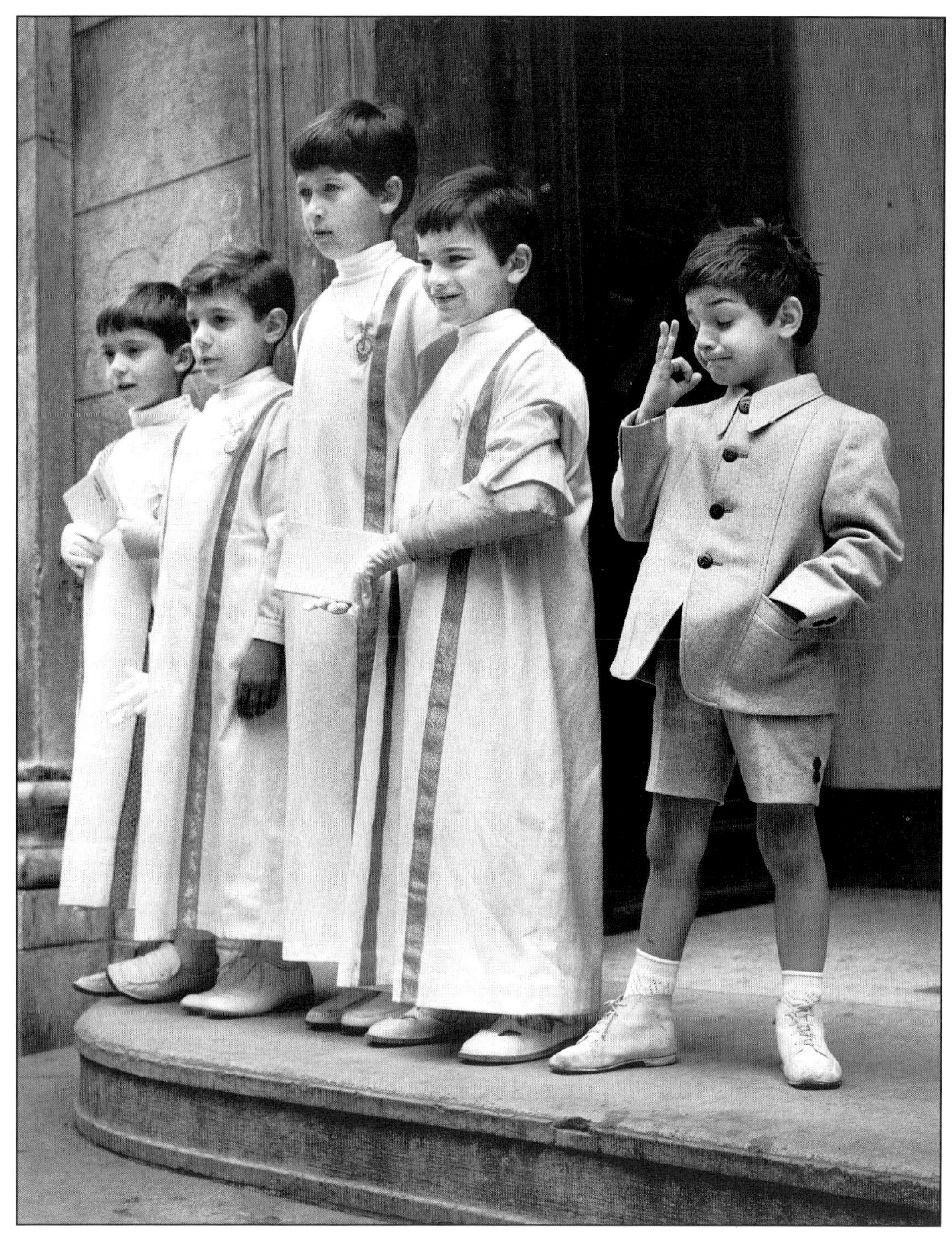

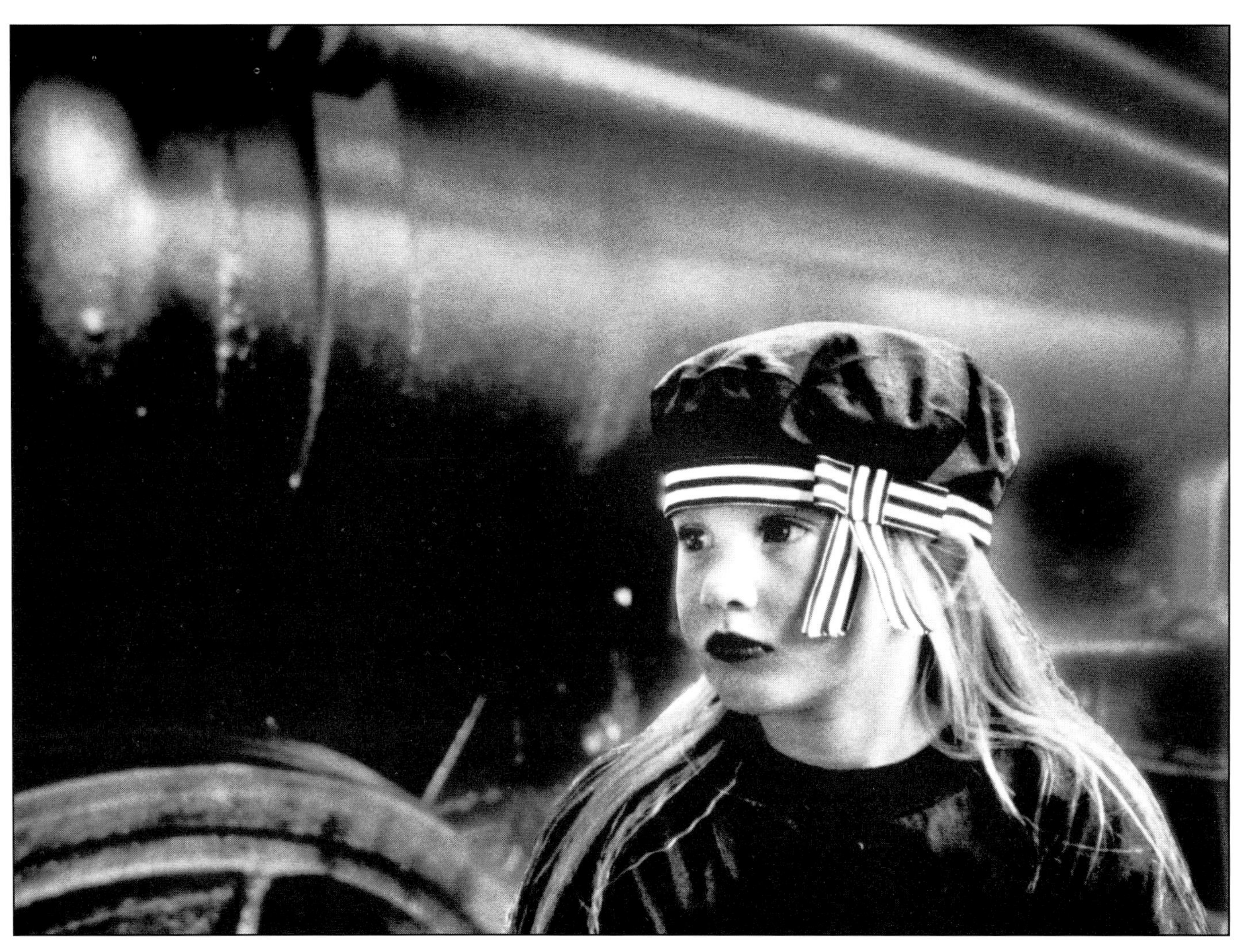

By the engine
montage

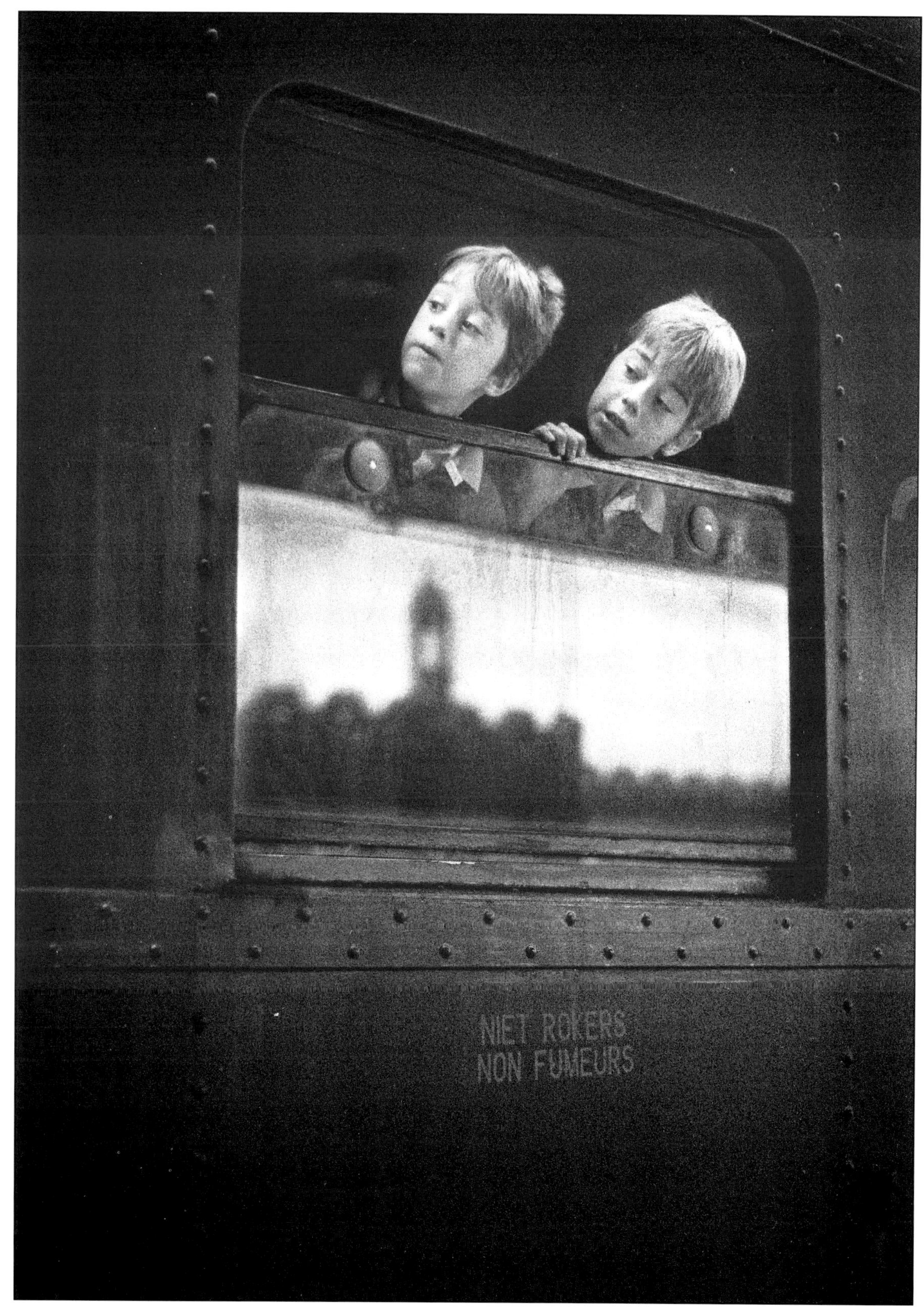

Train enthusiasts
Steam train weekend, Ghent, Belgium

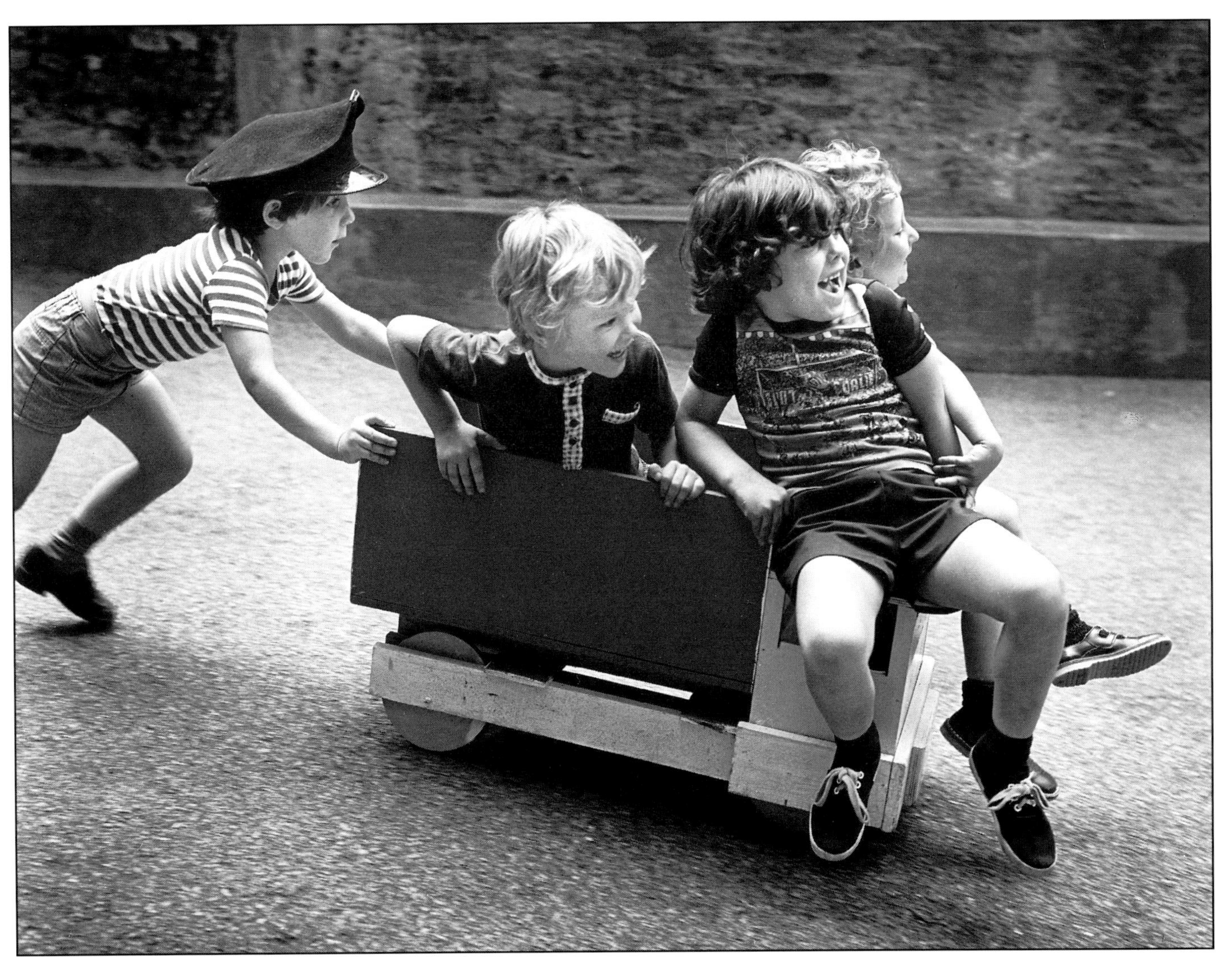

The playground express
Kensington playgroup, London

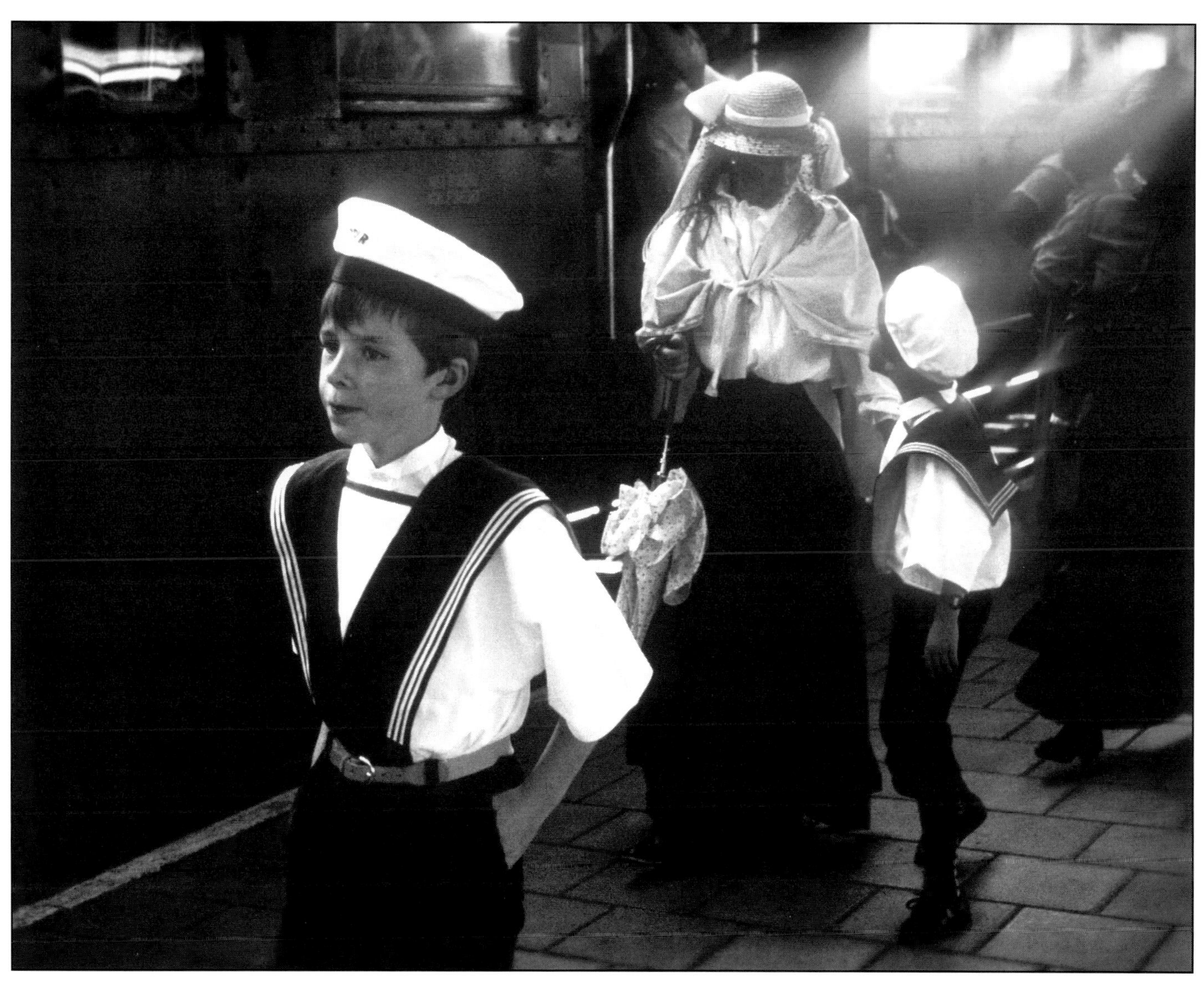

The railway children
Steam train event, Ghent, Belgium

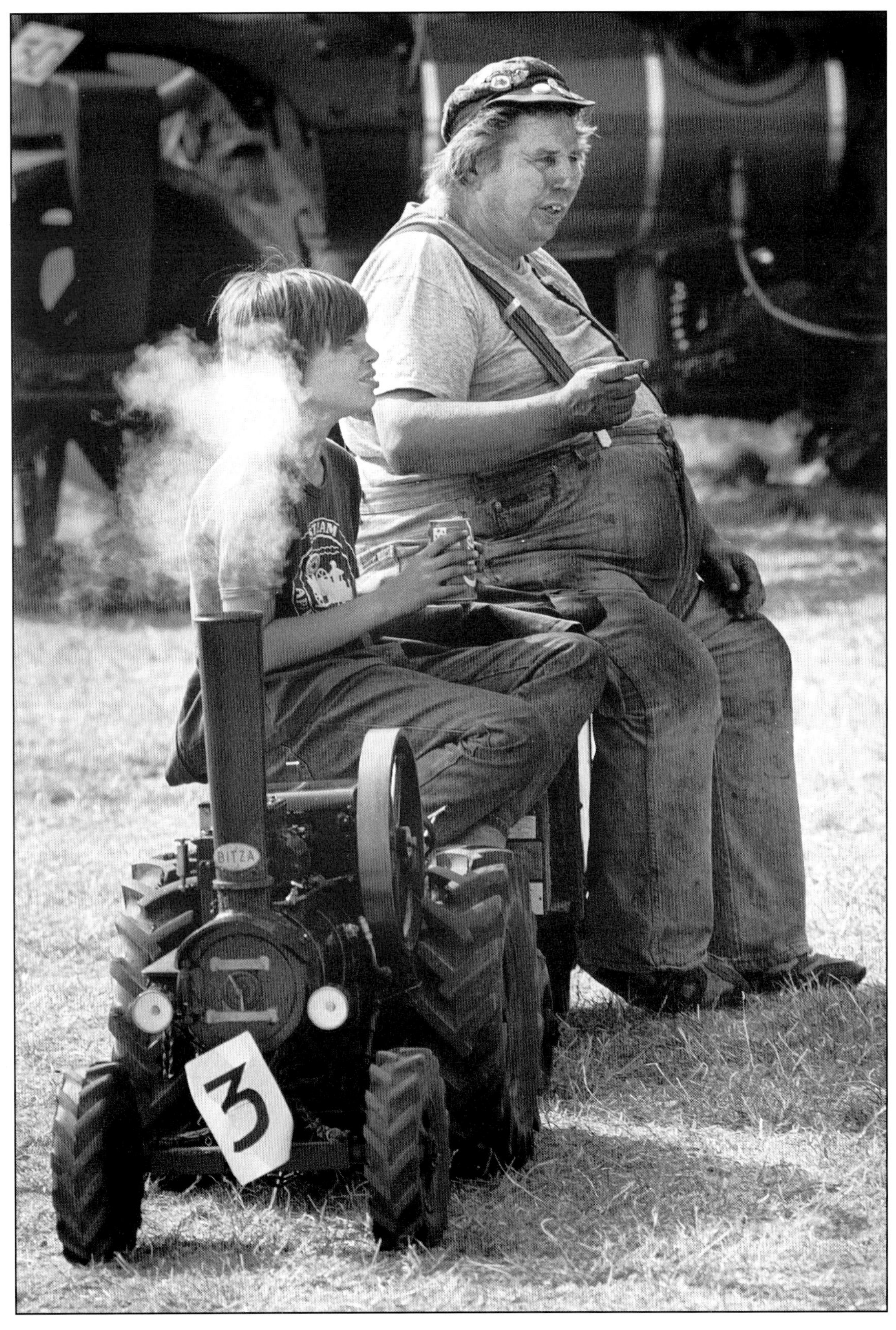

Enthusiasts for steam

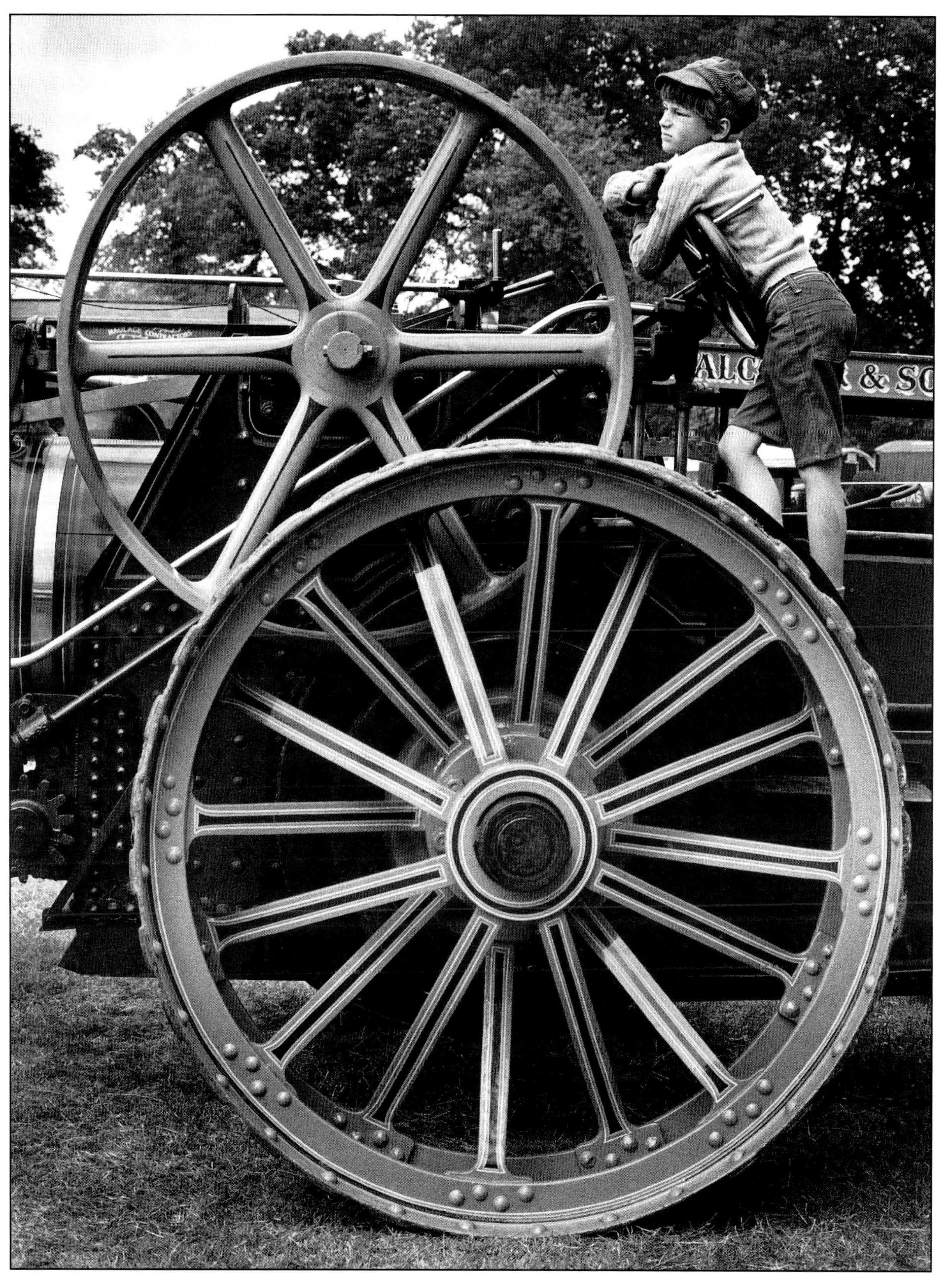

Big wheels
Brockley Park, London

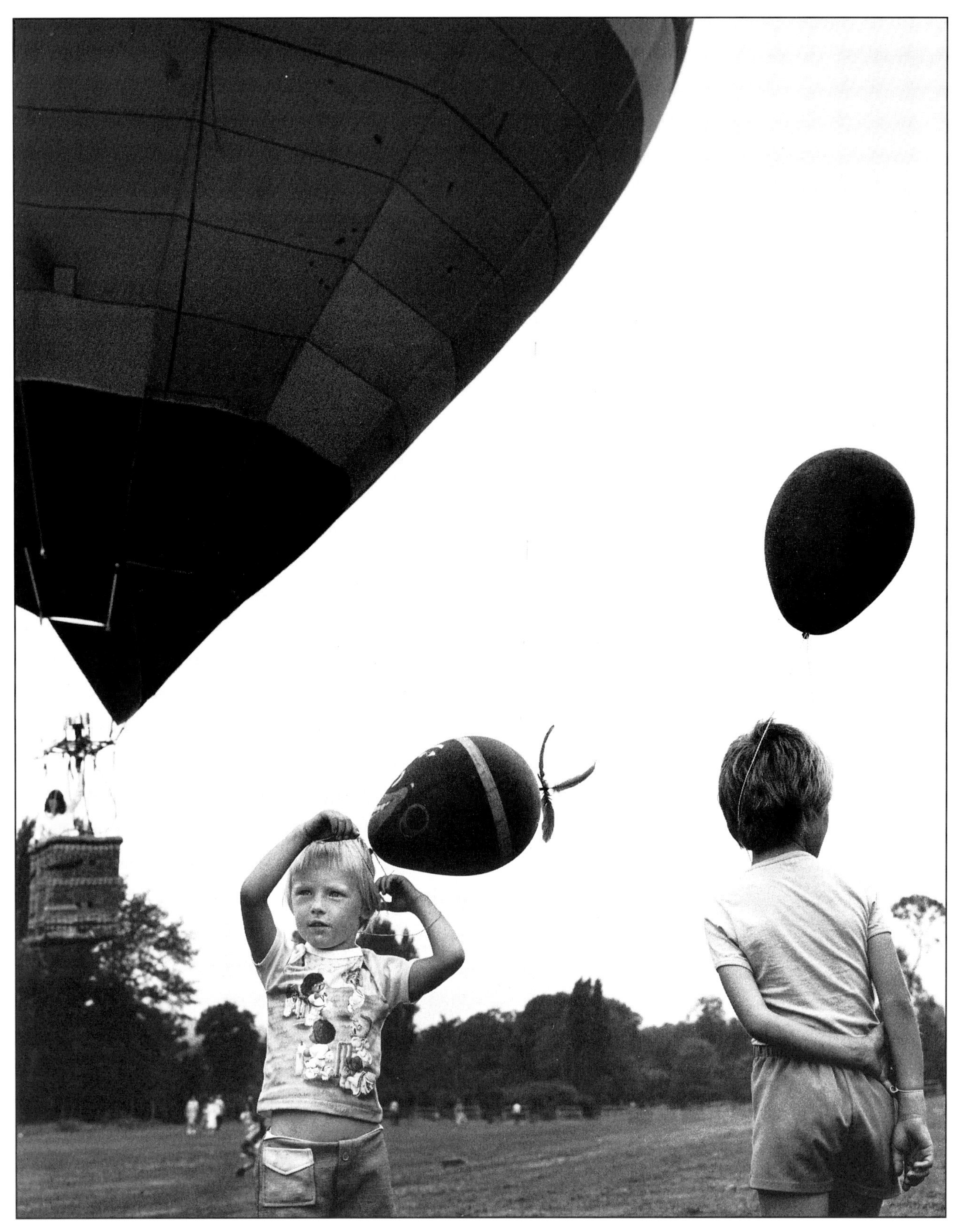

Balloons, big and small
Hampstead Heath, London

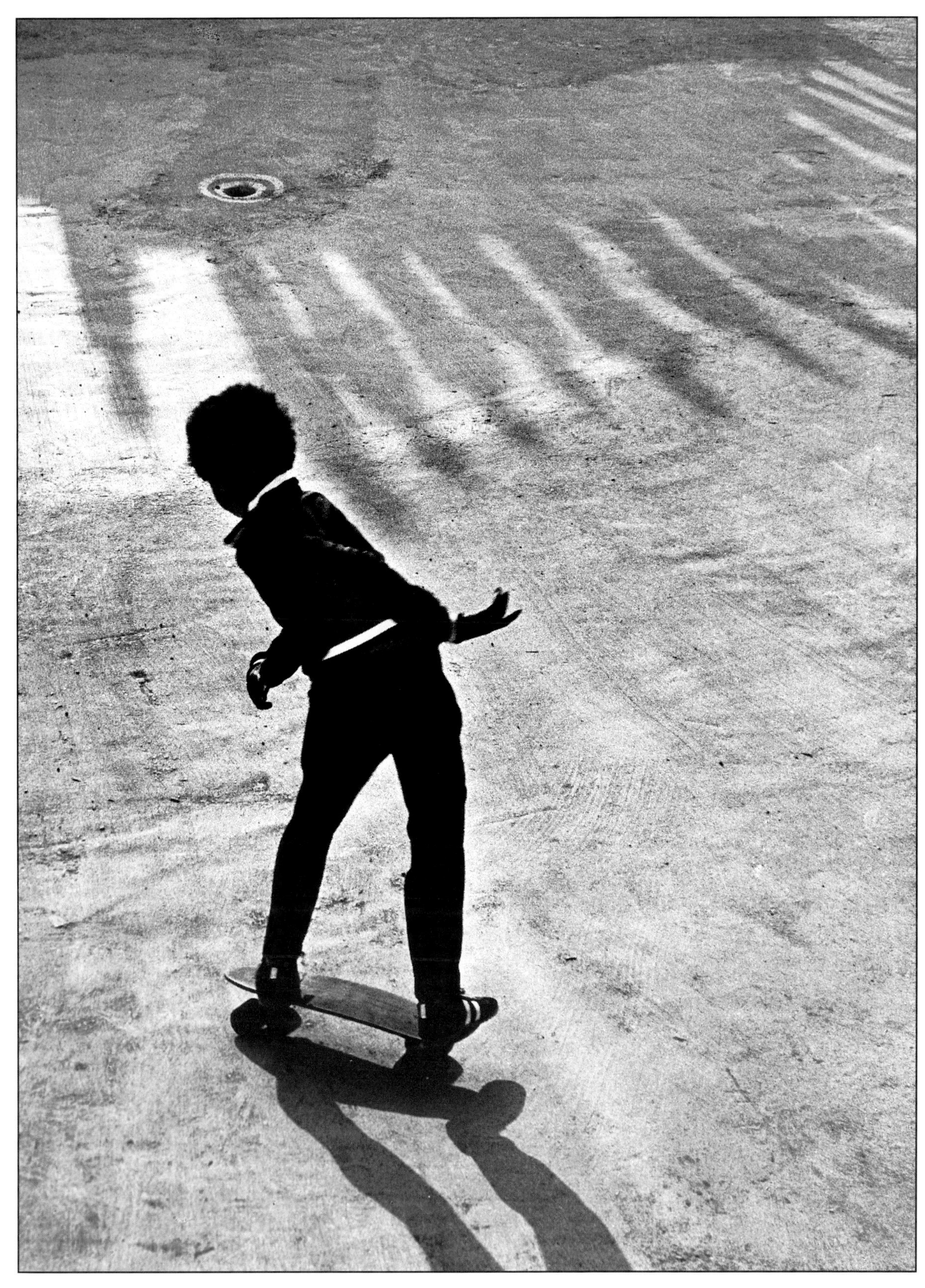

Playing to the crowd
Meanwhile Gardens, Kensington, London

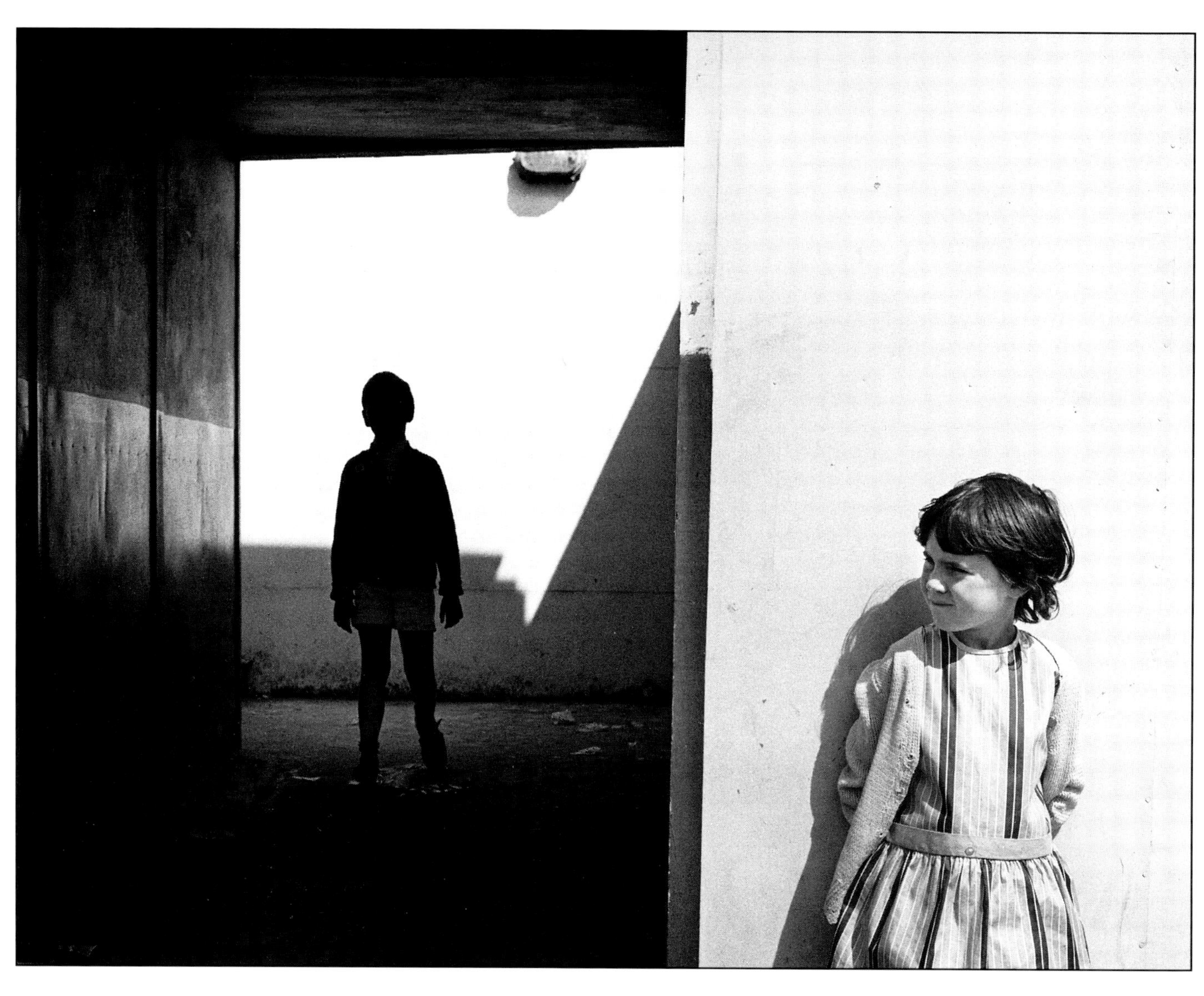

Boy and girl in the funfair
Barry Island, Wales

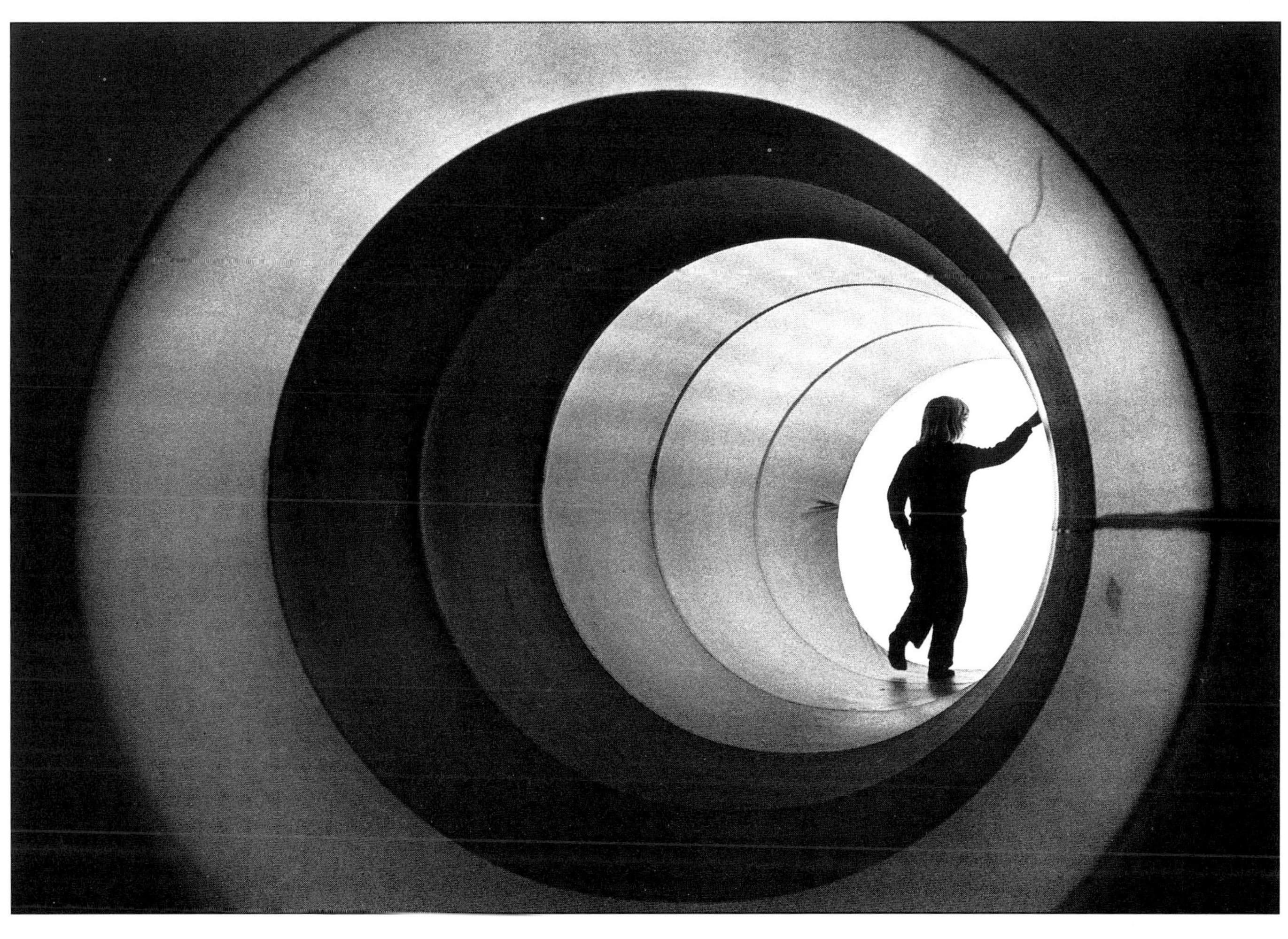

In the tunnel of an inflatable
Hampstead Heath, London

CARNIVAL

Carnival coming
Carnival here
Floats and music
Parties and beer

Carnival noisy
Carnival loud
Blow your whistle
Flow with the crowd

Carnival happy
Carnival wild
Bang that drum
Colourful child

Carnival ending
Carnival gone
Keep the dream
And life goes on.

Elia Morreg

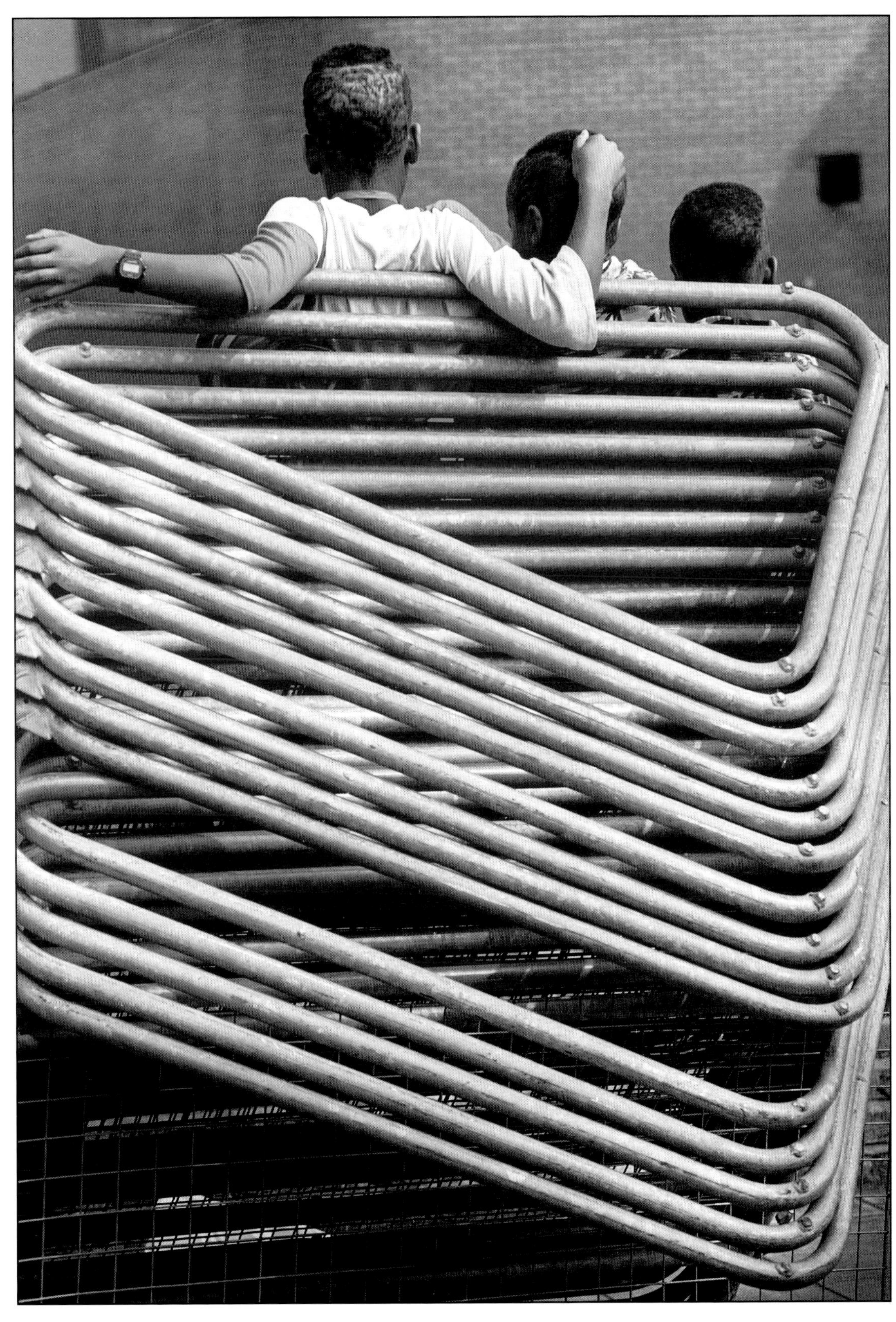

Boys resting on the barriers
Notting Hill carnival, London

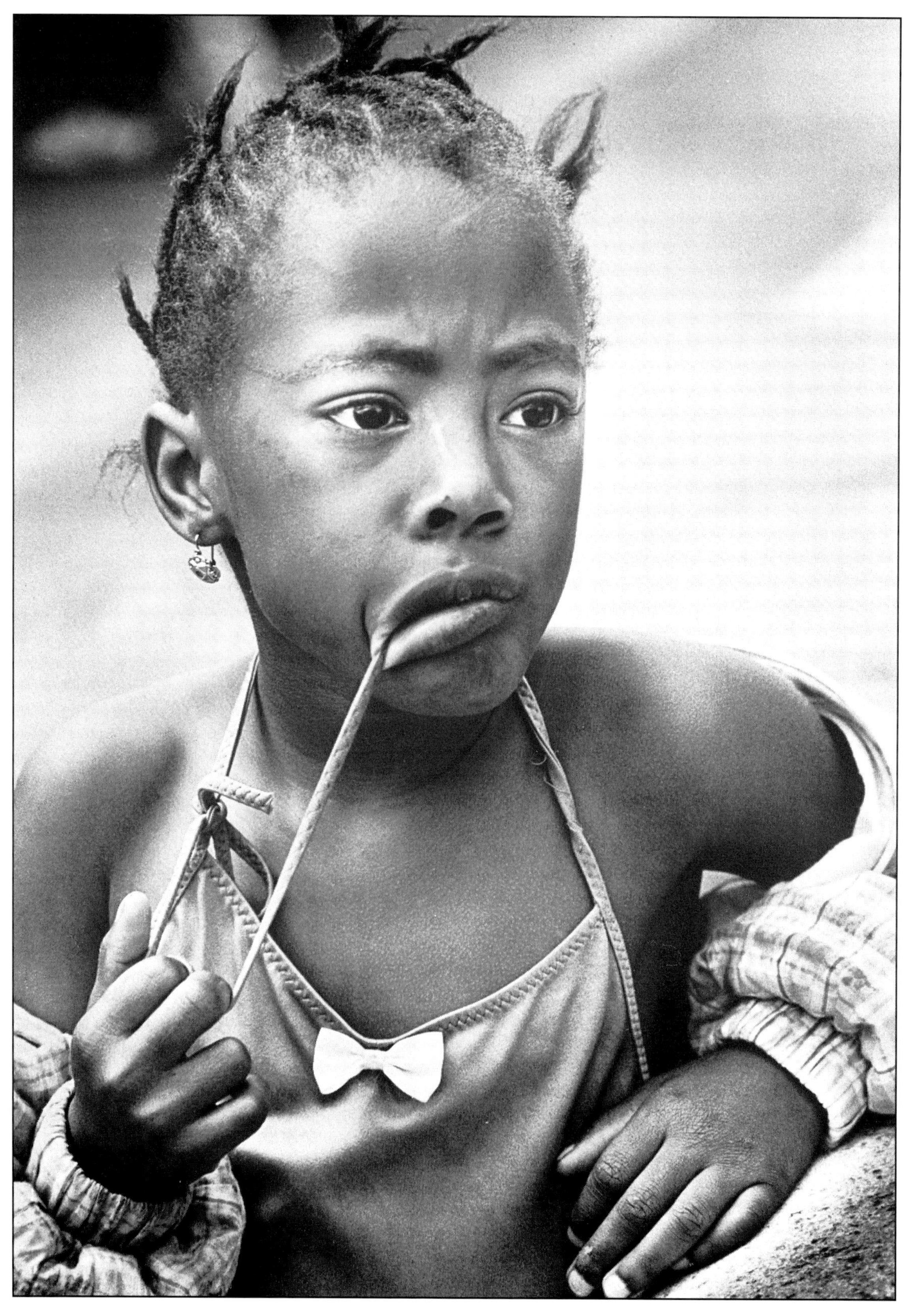

Strap chewer
Notting Hill carnival, London

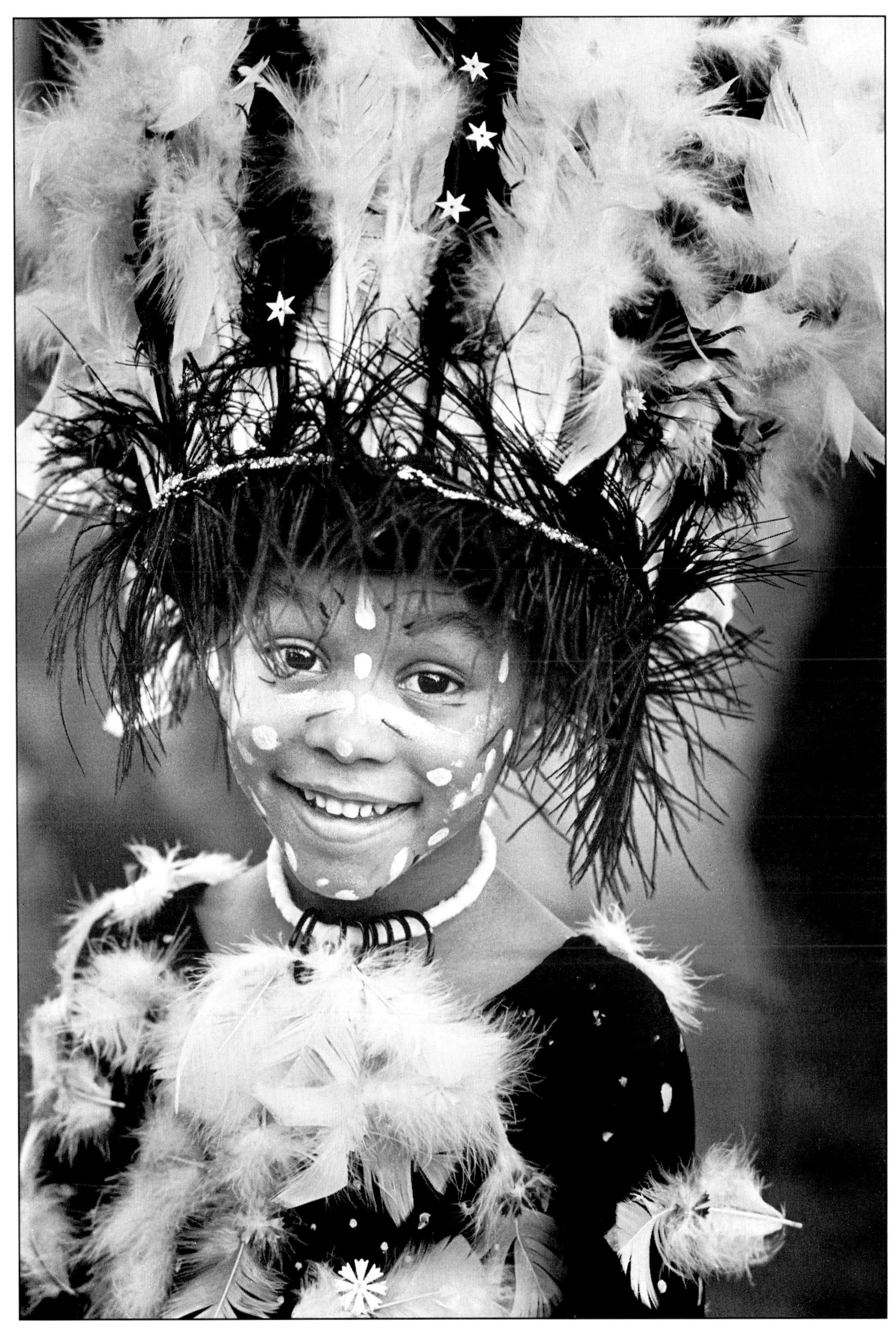

Forty thousand feathers
Notting Hill carnival, London

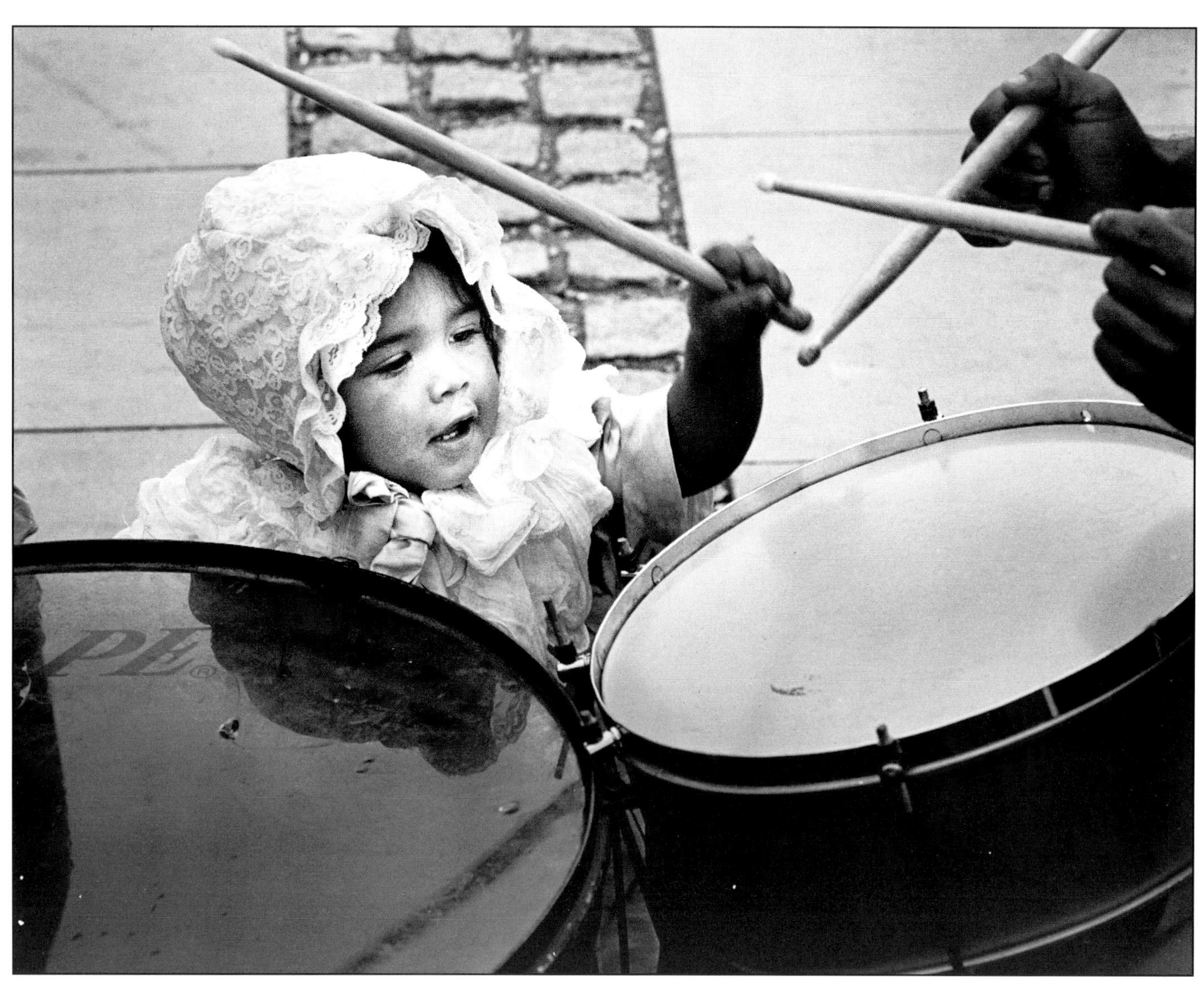

A very little drummer girl
Richmond, Surrey

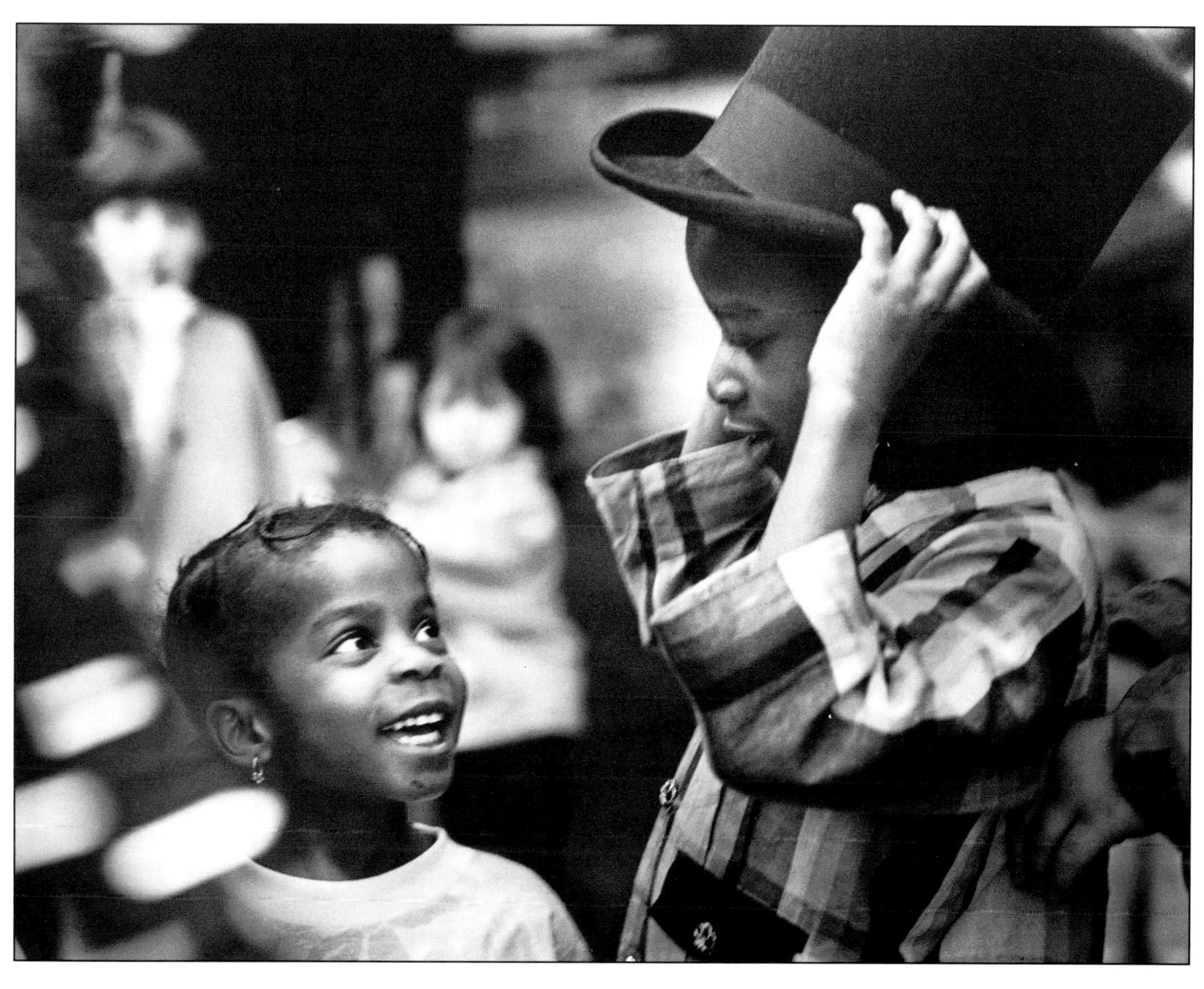

Top hat game
Grimaldi festival, Euston, London

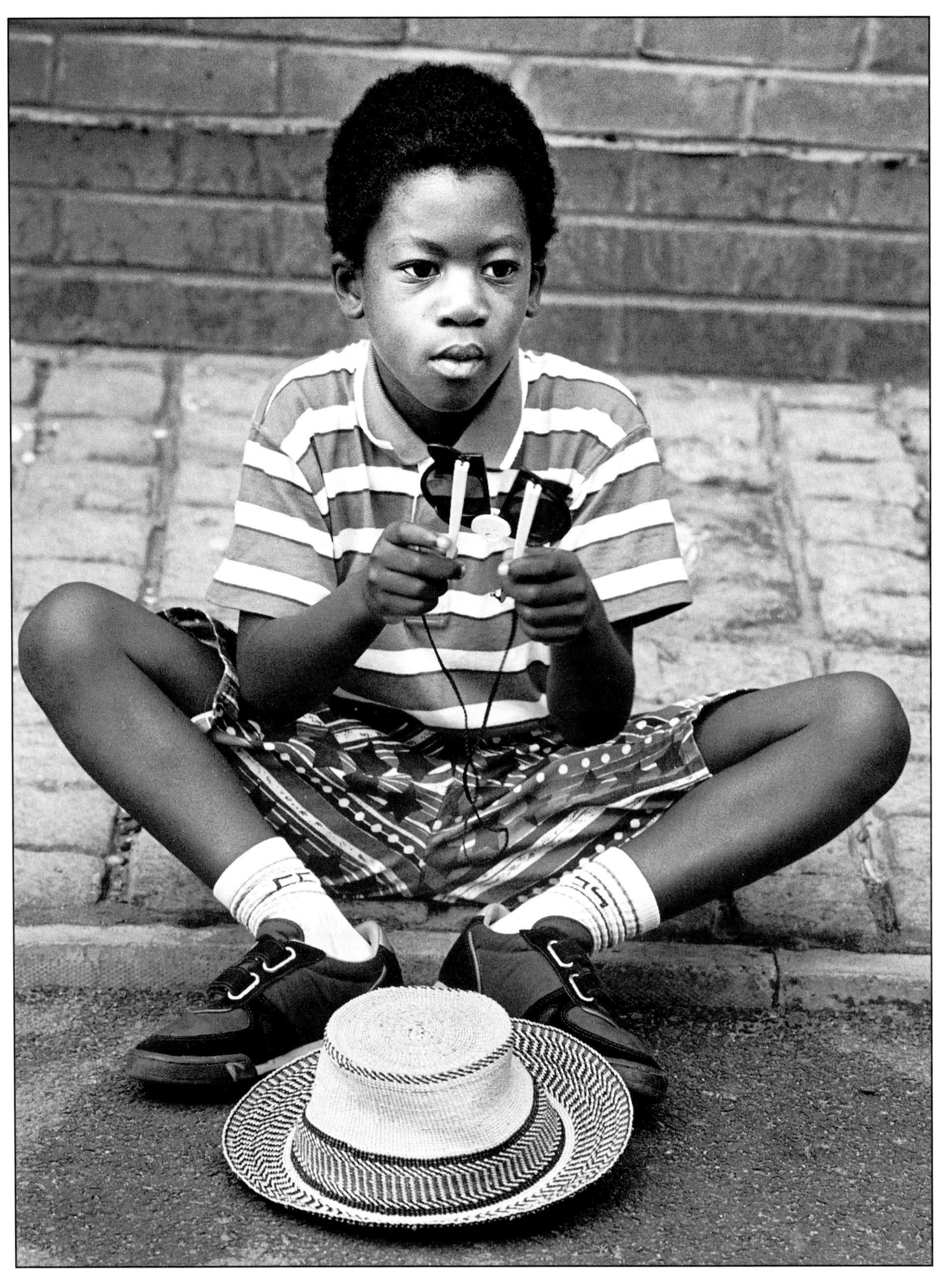

Waiting for the parade
Notting Hill carnival, London

50

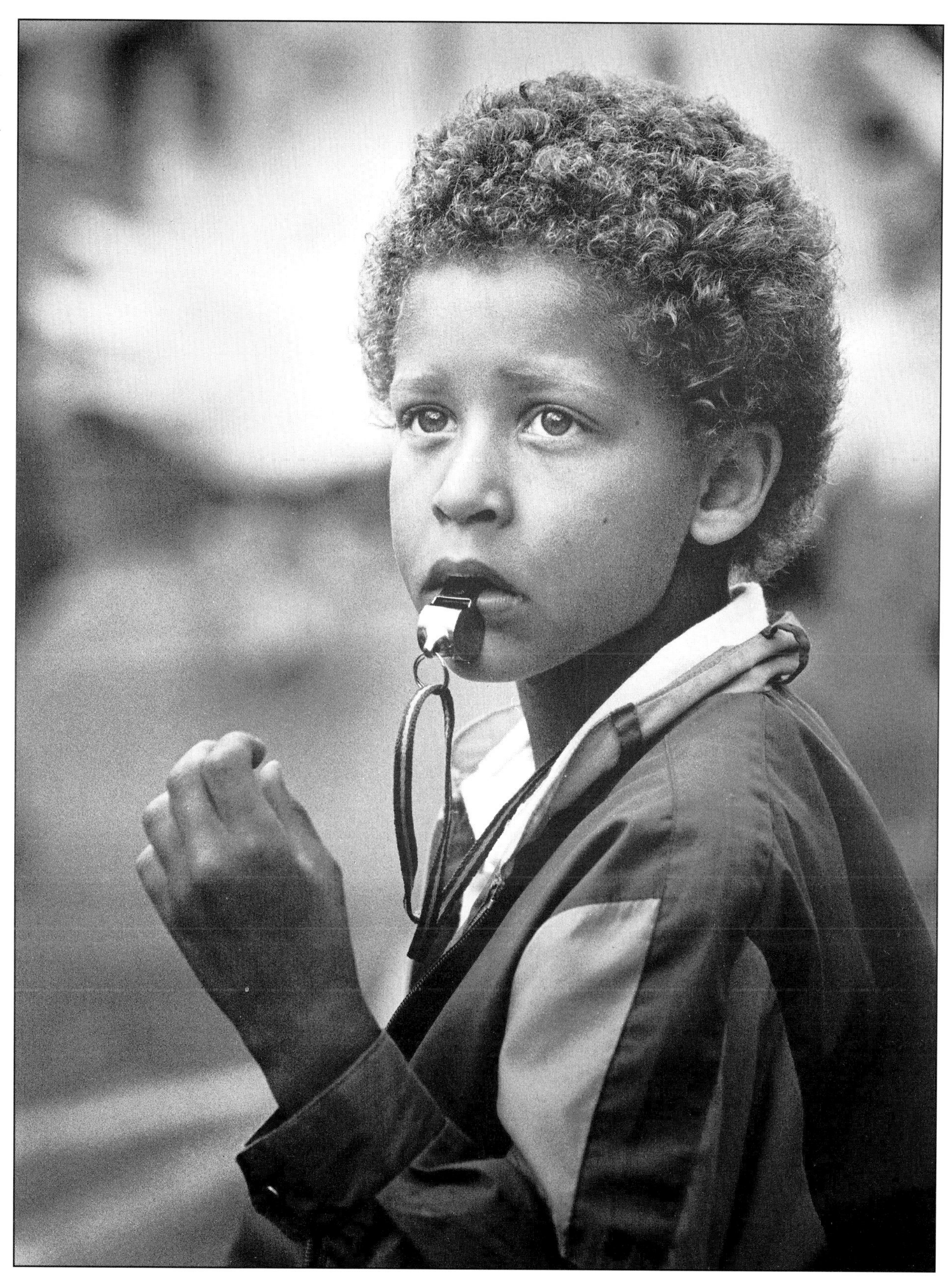

Whistler
Notting Hill carnival, London

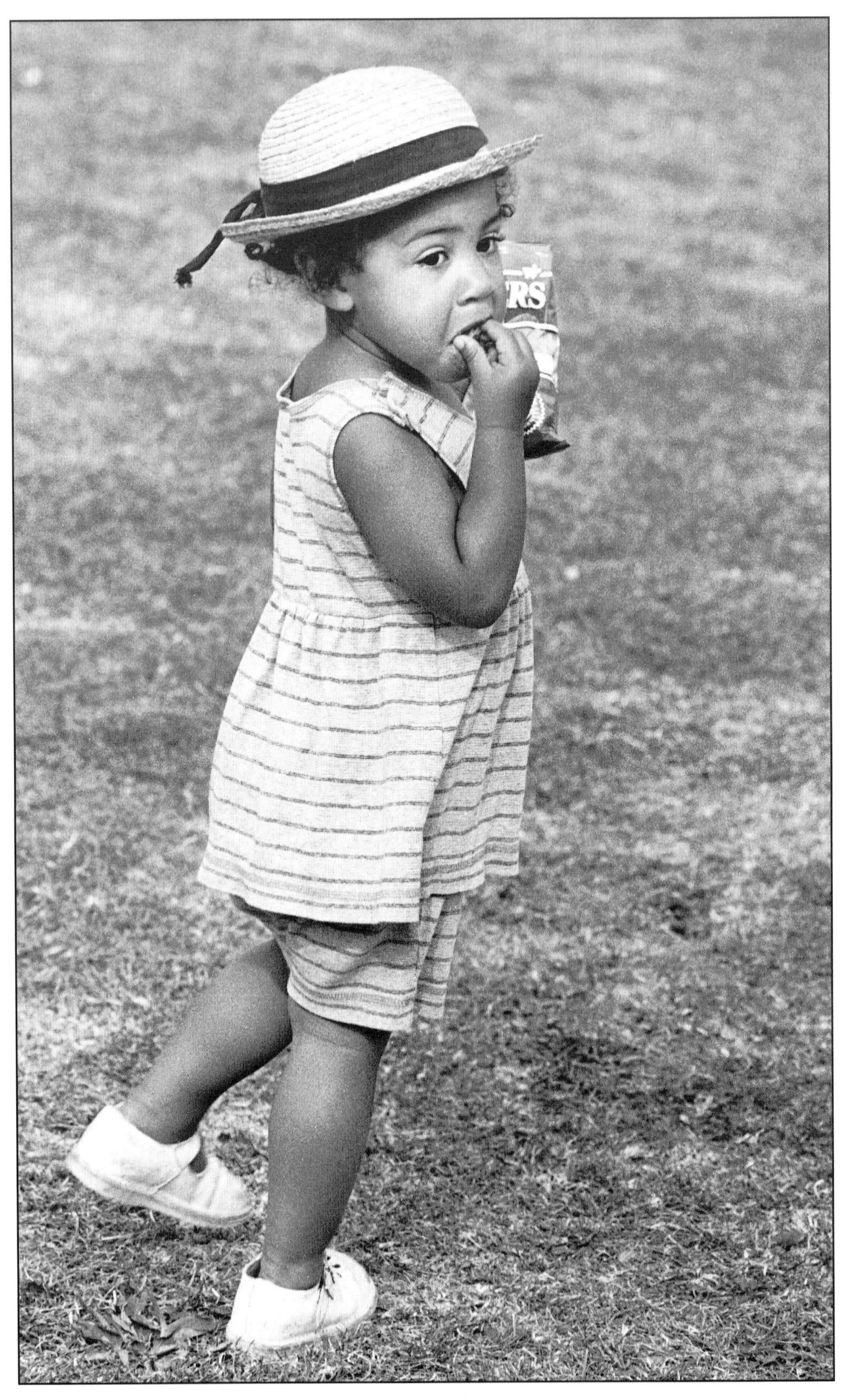

Stopping for a snack
Battersea Park, London

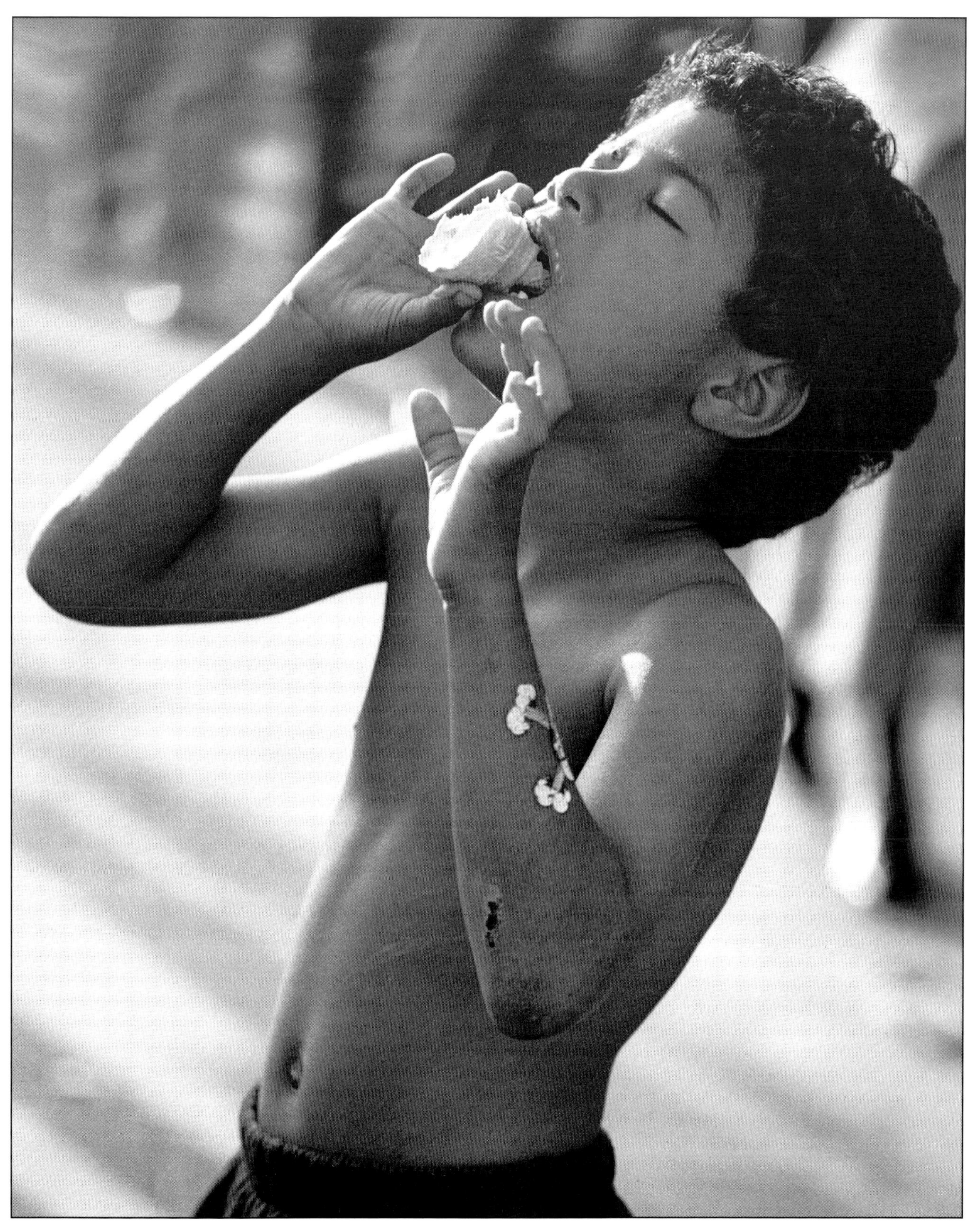

Ice cream delight
Kensal Road, London

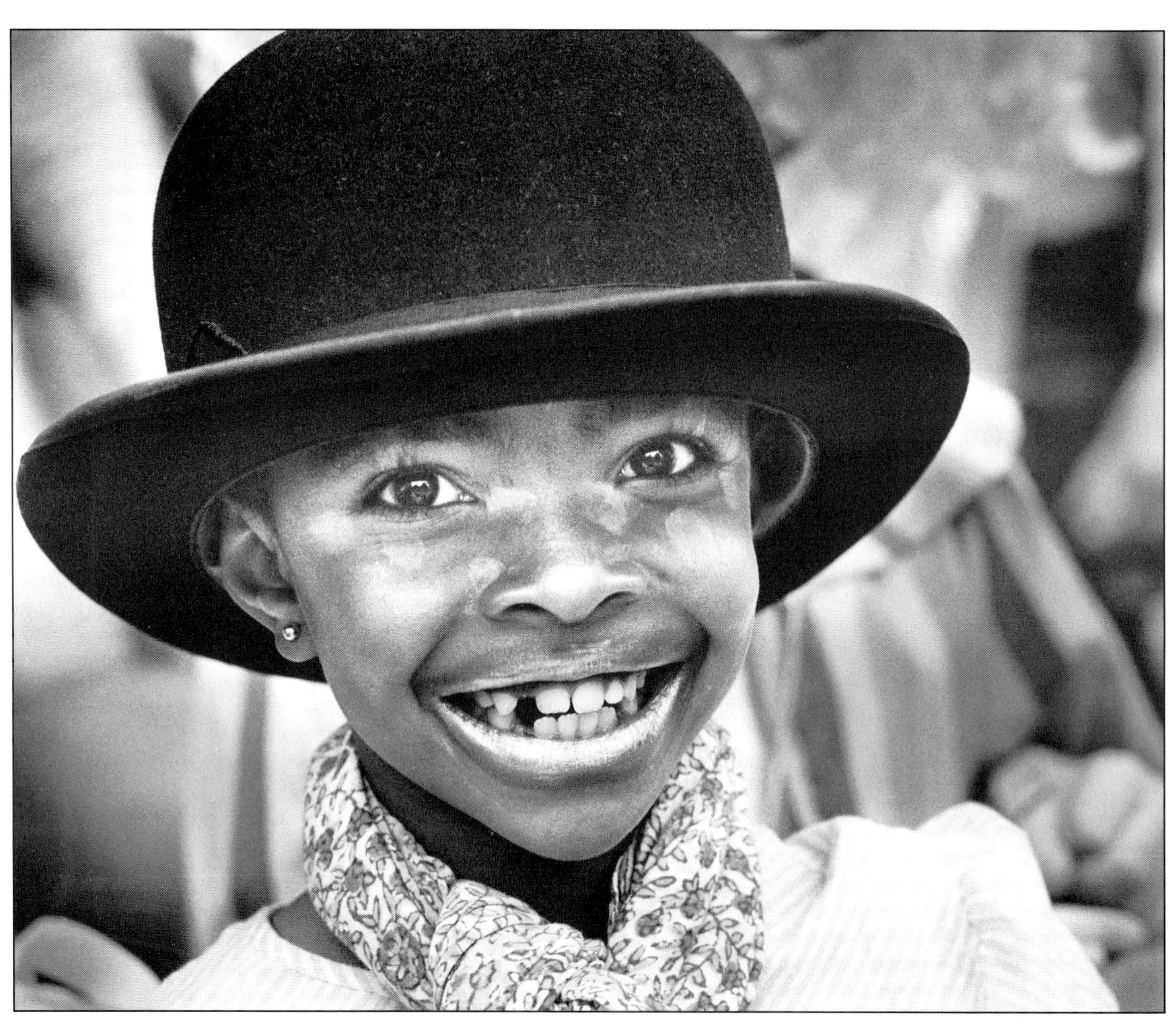

Happy hatter
Chalcot Square fair, London

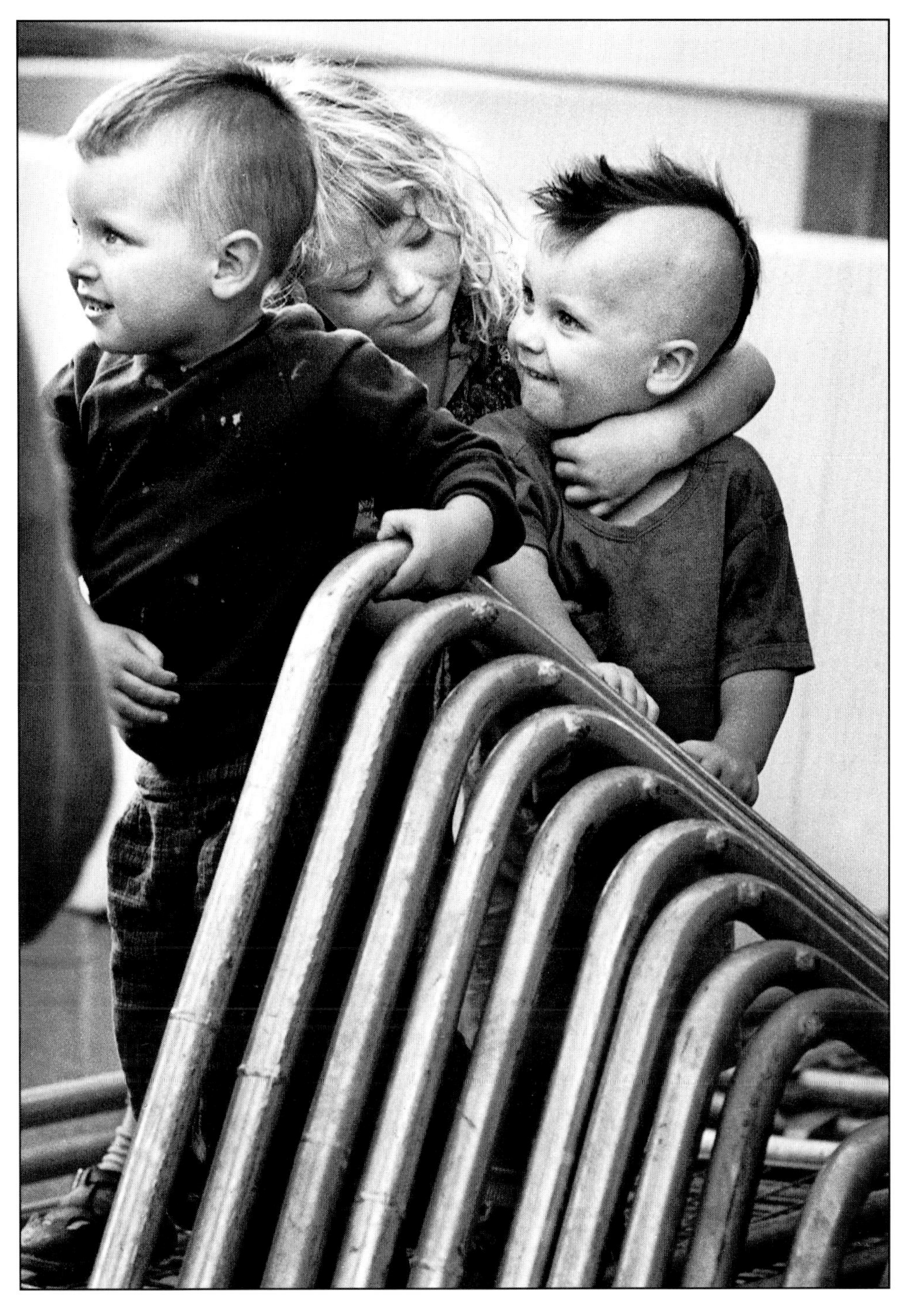

Barrier trio
Outside the Festival Hall, London

MONDAY'S CHILD

Monday's child is fair of face,
Tuesday's child is full of grace,
Wednesday's child is full of woe,
Thursday's child has far to go,
Friday's child is loving and giving,
Saturday's child works hard for his living,
And the child that is born on a Sunday
Is fair and wise, and good and gay.

Traditional

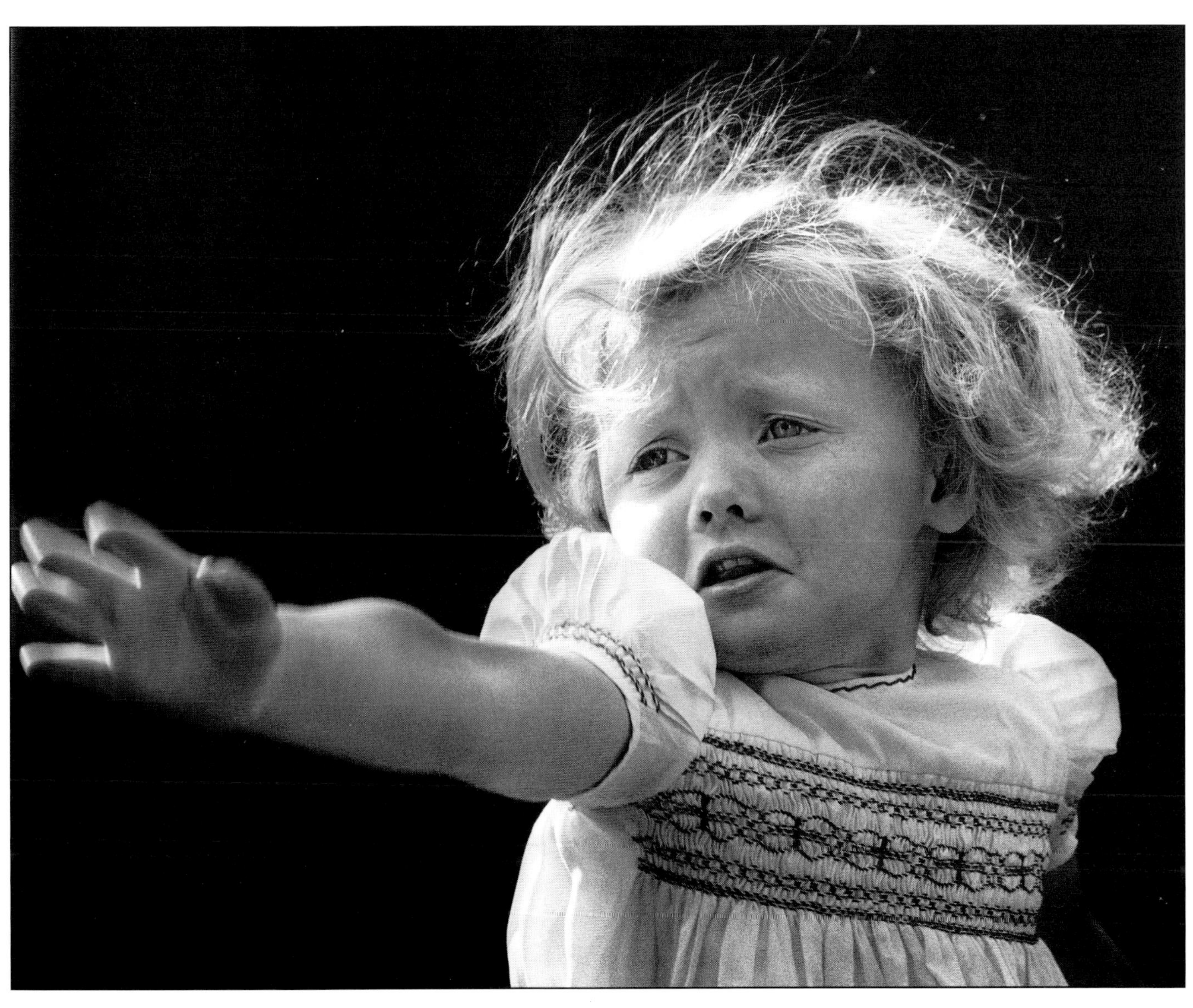

"That's mine"
Crowthorne, Berkshire

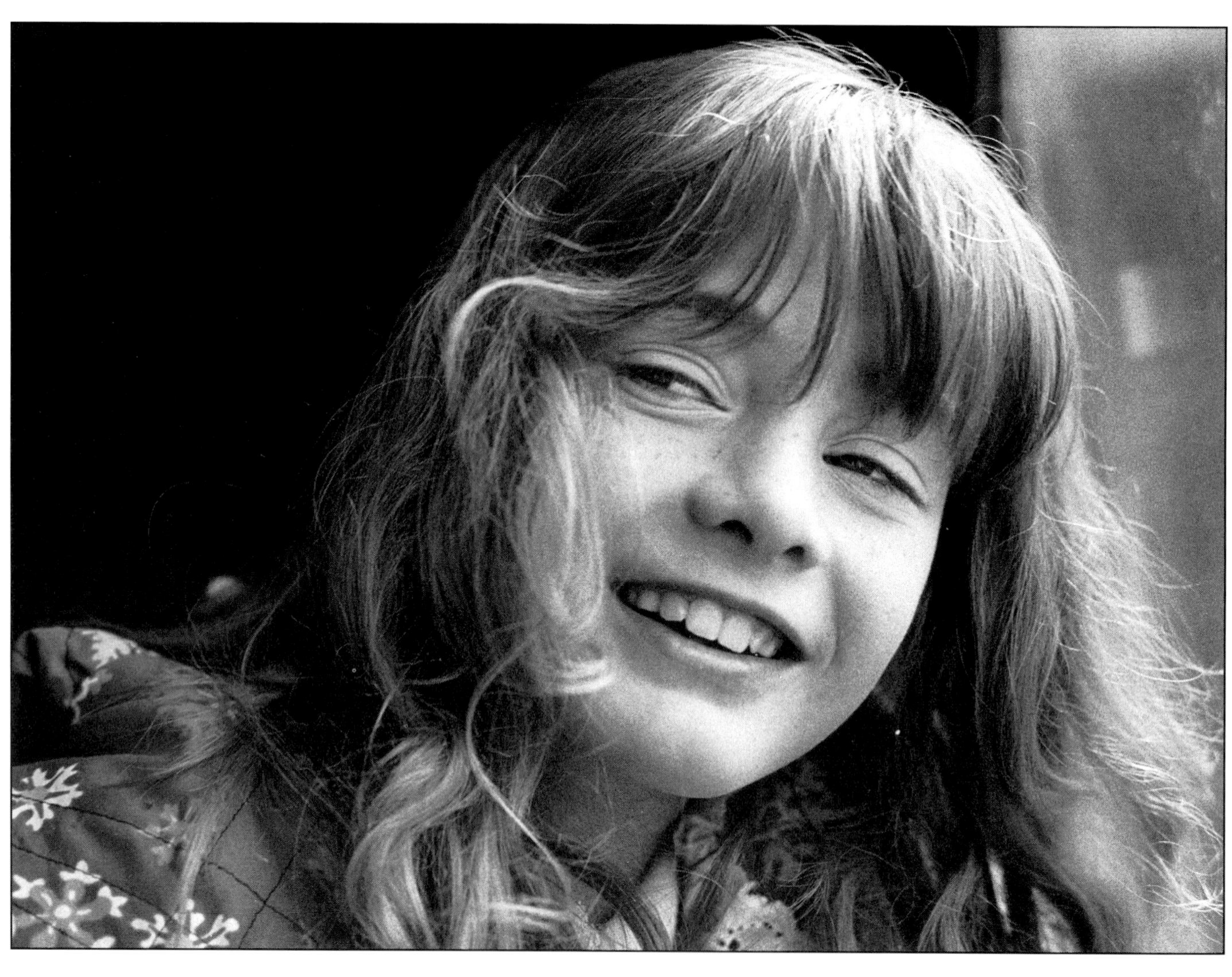

Claire (" with an 'e' ")
On the train to Waterloo, London

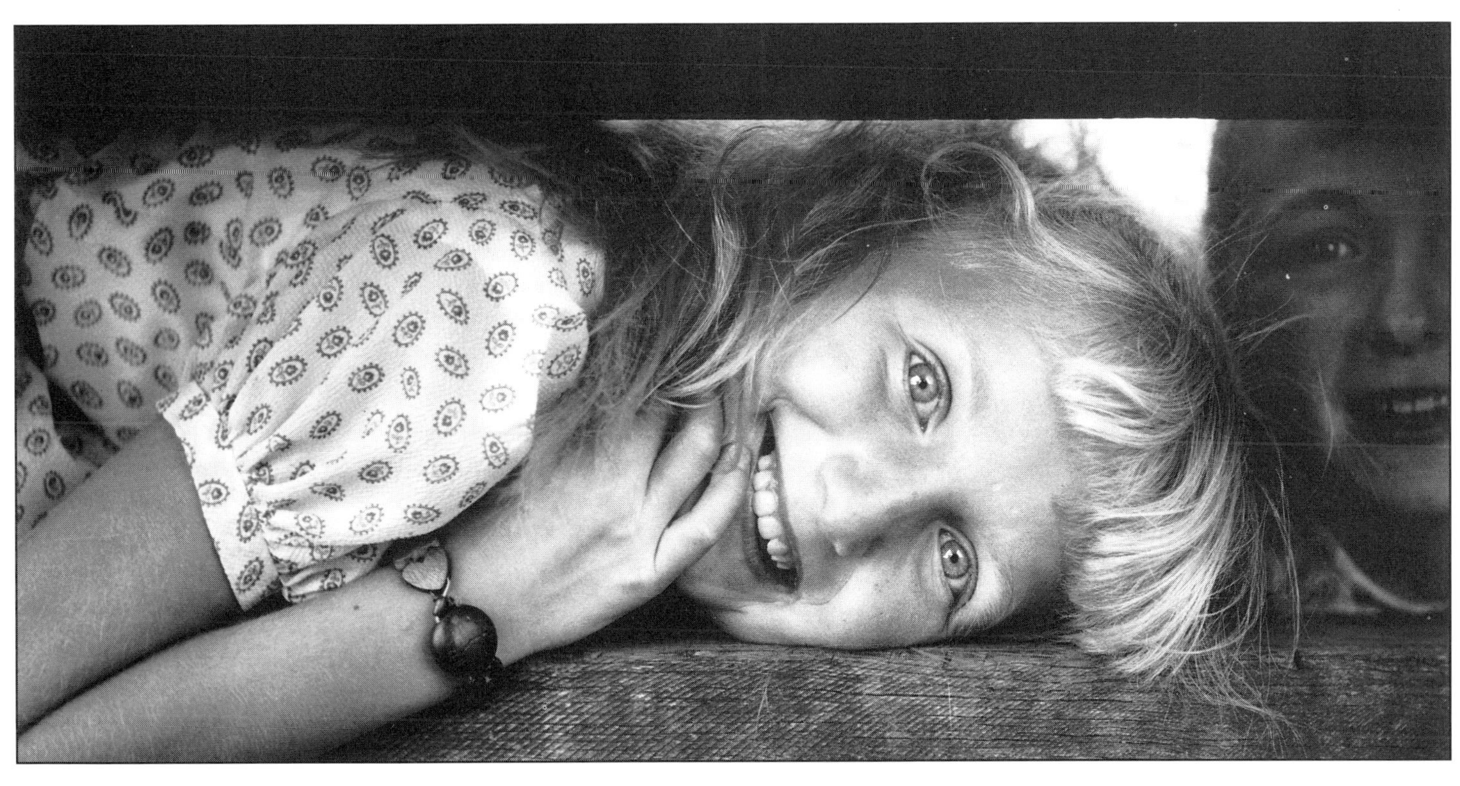

***Between the steps of the old windmill**
Bruges, Belgium*

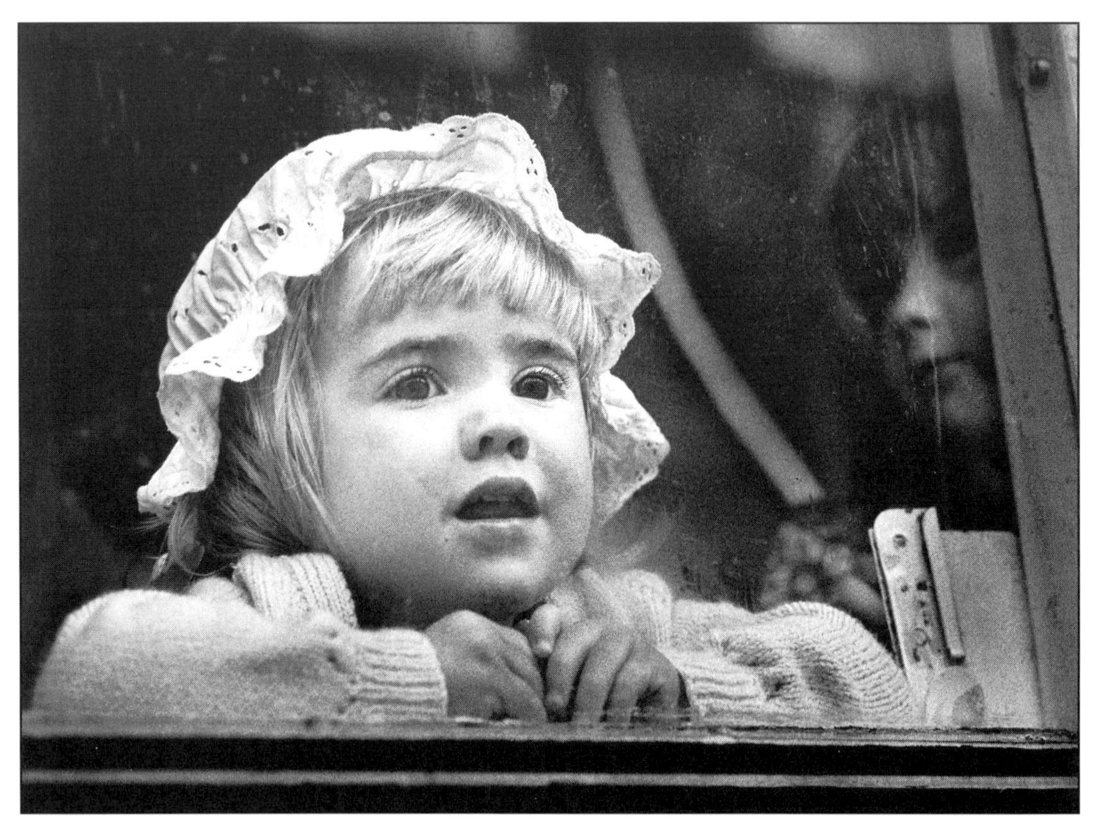

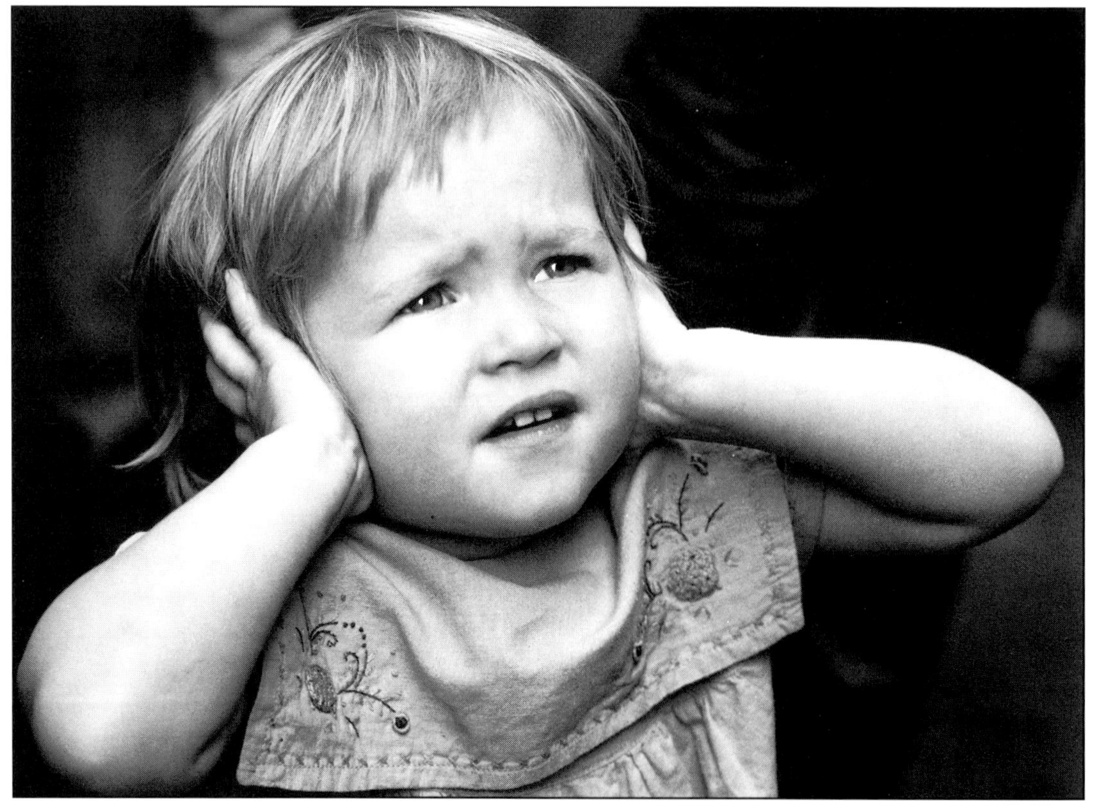

(top) **At the window of a bus**, *Chalcot Square, London*
(below) **"I can't listen"**, *Punch and Judy show, London*

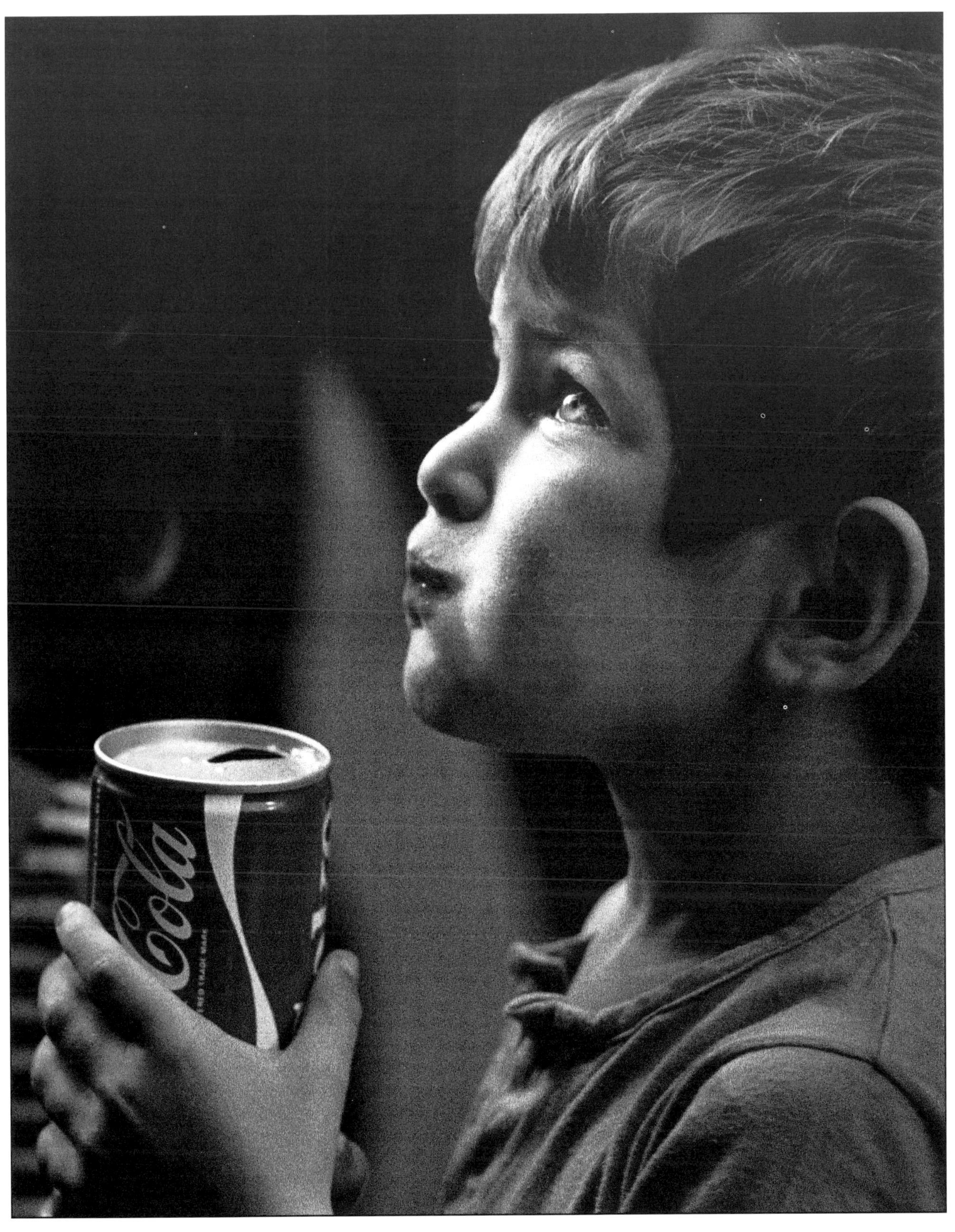

Cola boy
Punch and Judy show, London

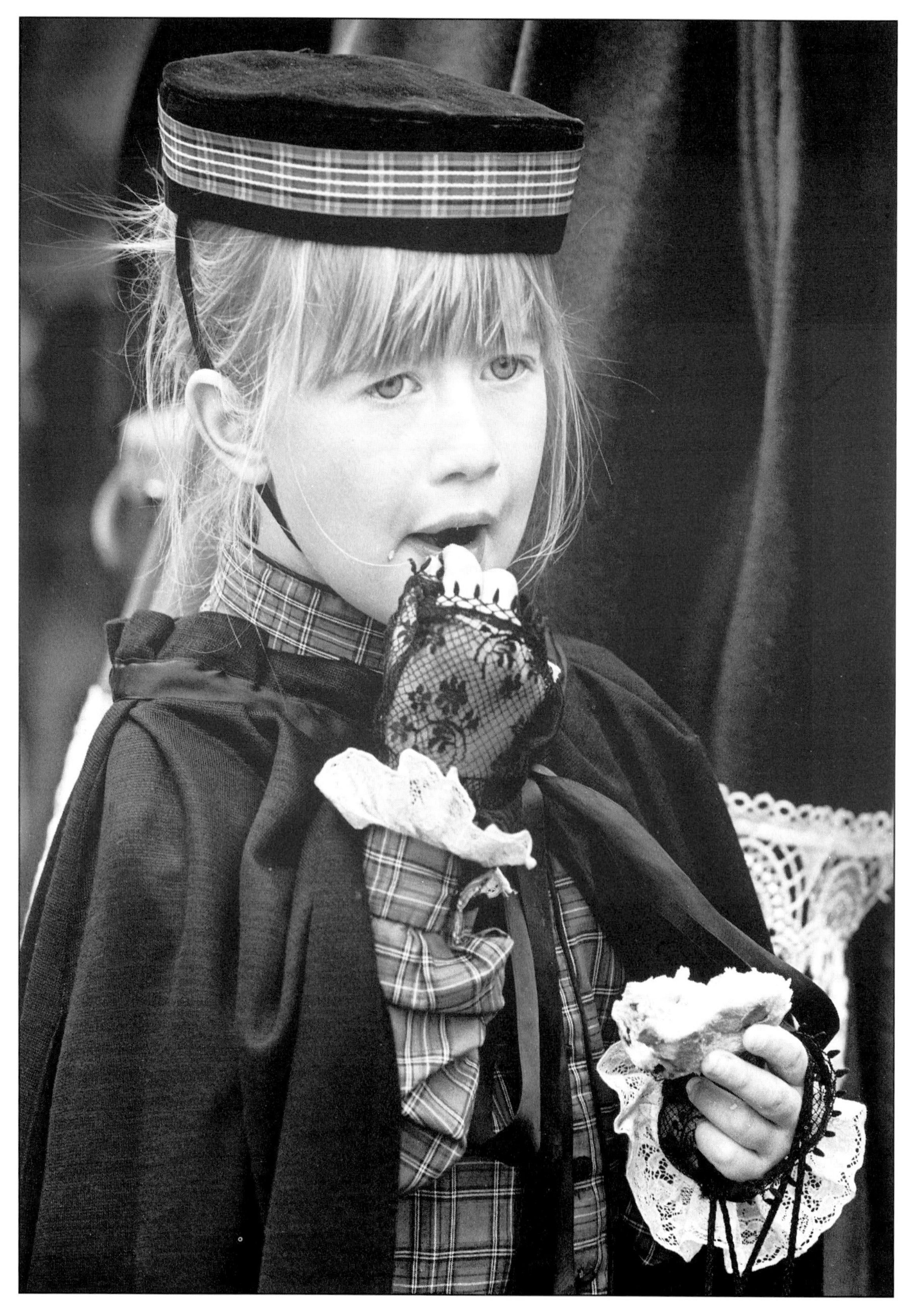

Girl at the Dickens festival
Rochester, Kent

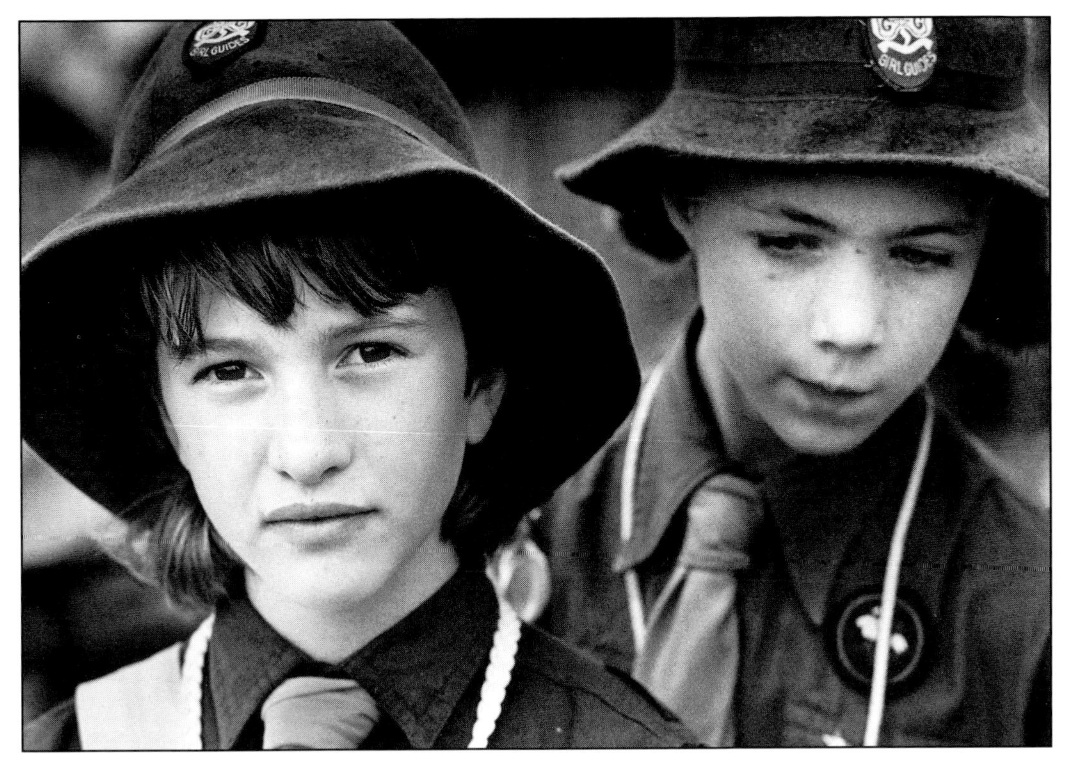

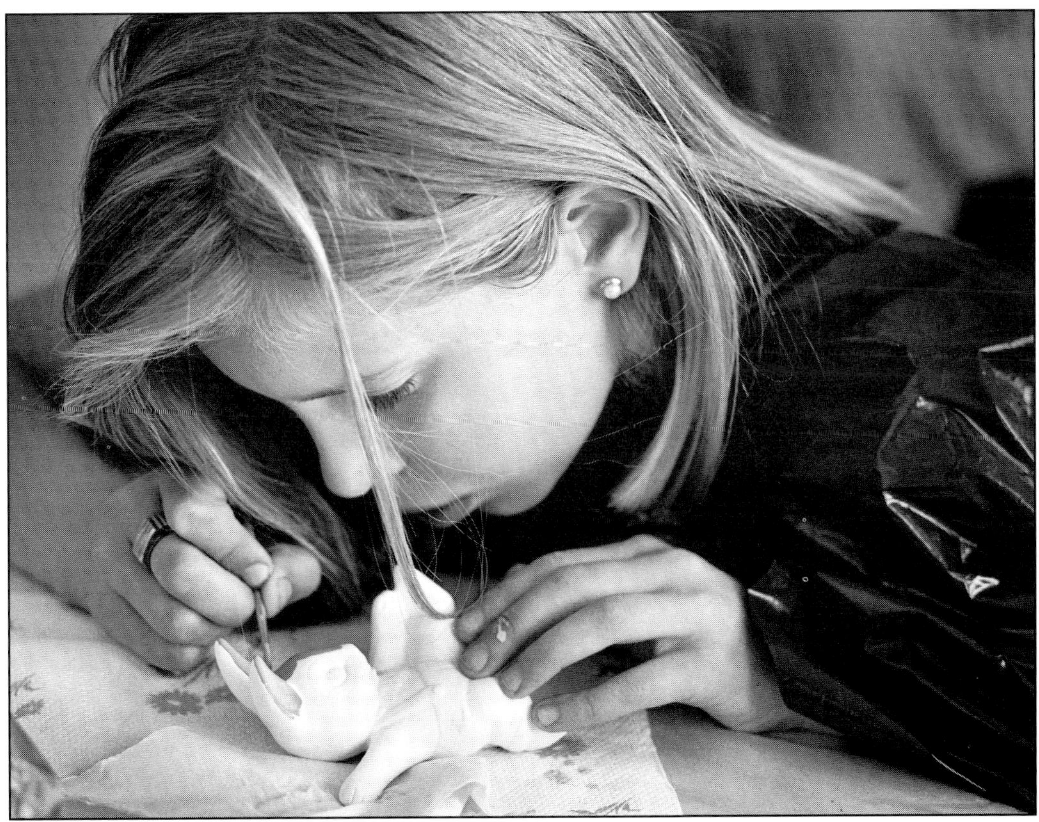

(top) **Guides in 1920s style uniforms,** *Newbury, Berkshire*
(below) **Painting a rabbit,** *Syon Park craft fair*

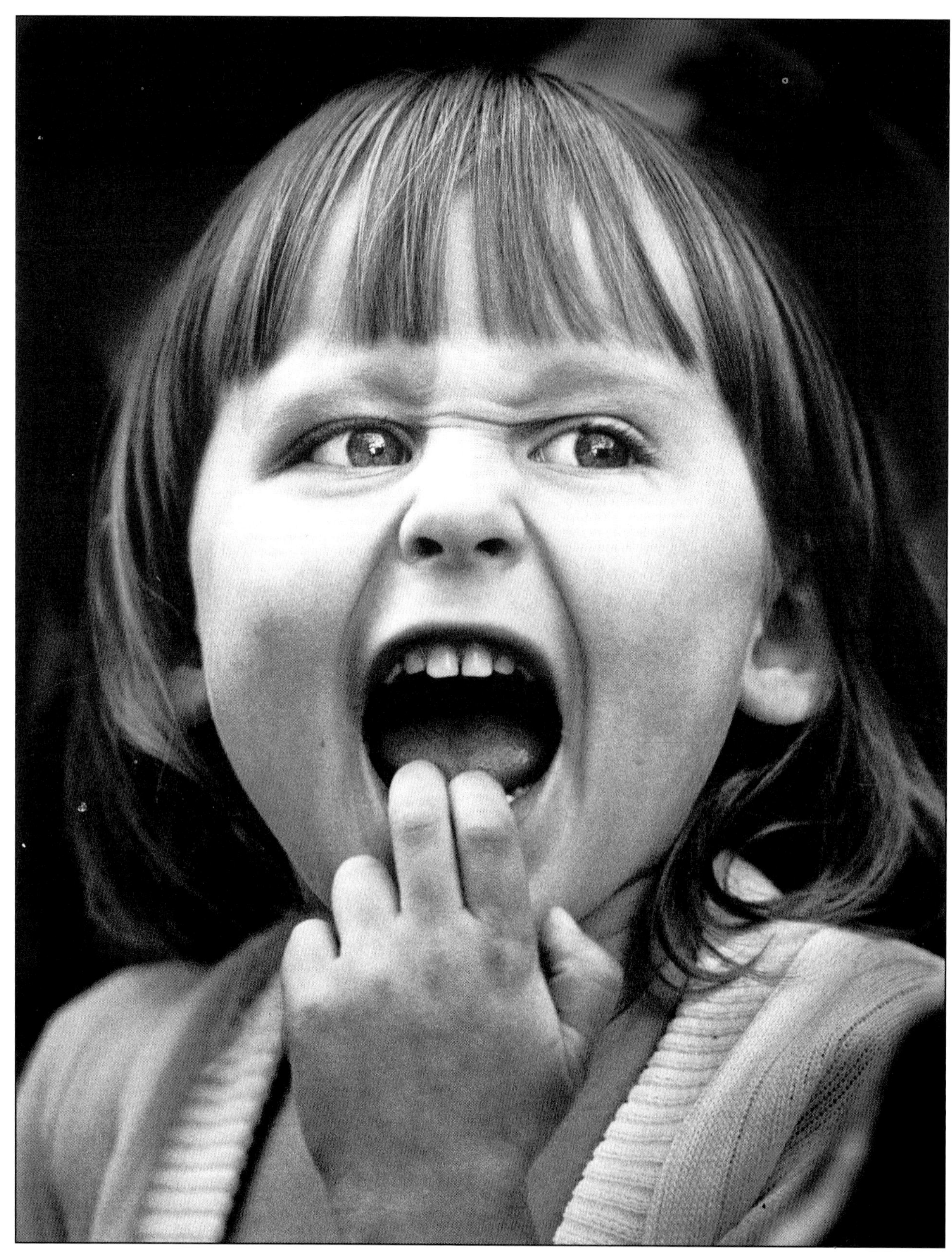

Reaction to Mr Punch
Covent Garden, London

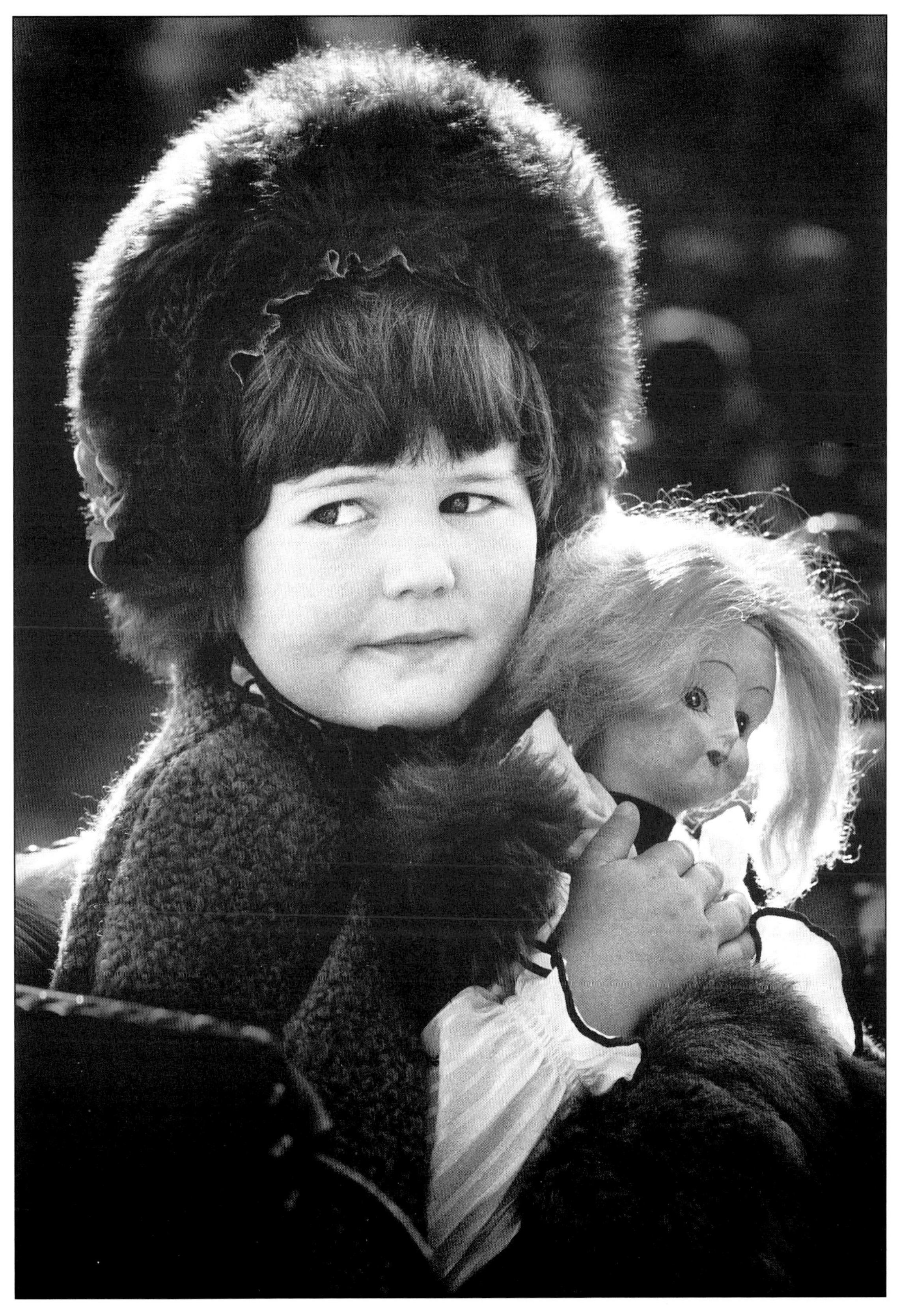

Girl in a fur hat
Victorian carriage parade, Hyde Park, London

Childhood should surely be
A time of happy memory;
But sadly 'tis not always thus.

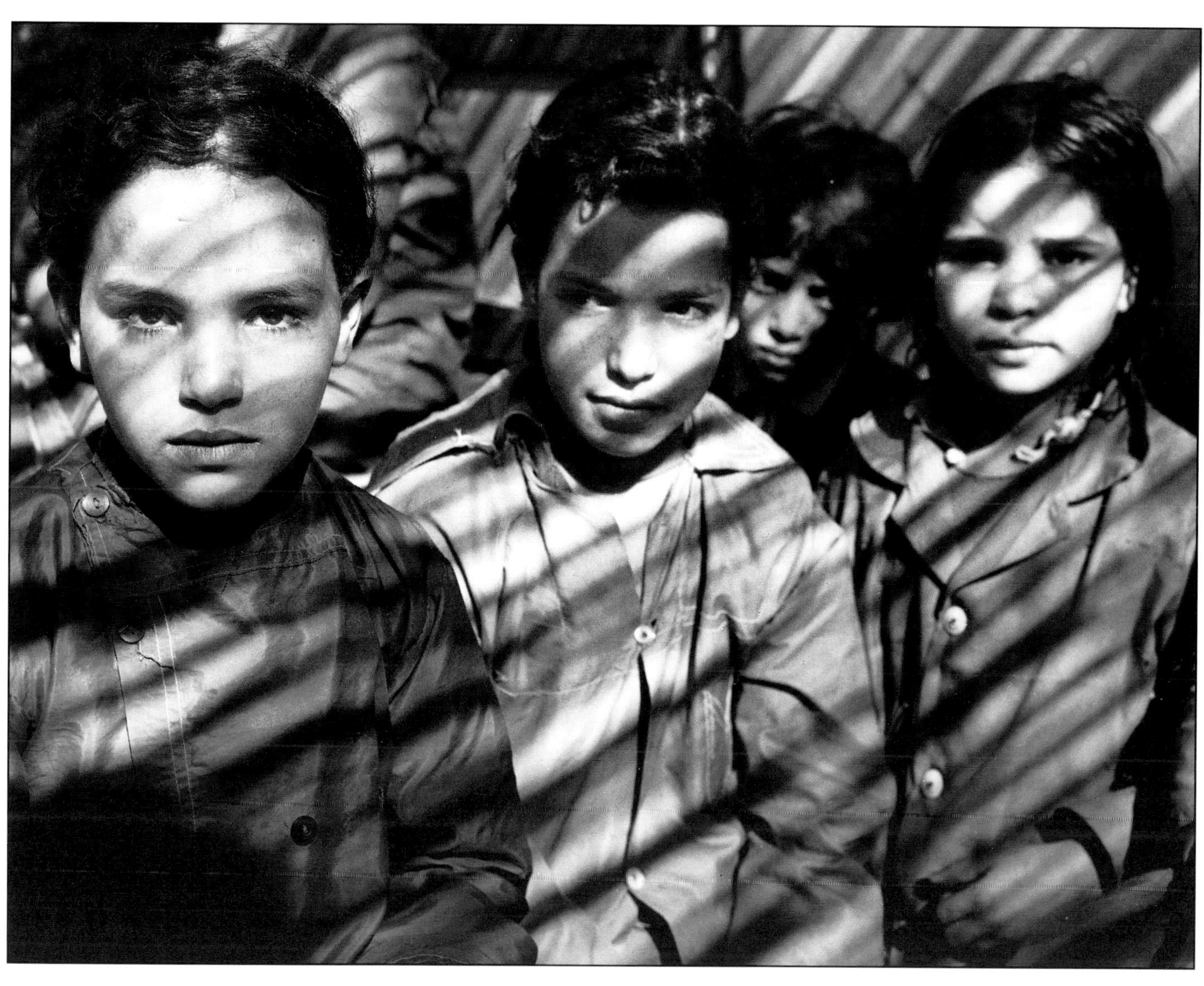

Needlework trainees awaiting a Save the Children Fund hot meal
Agadir, Morocco

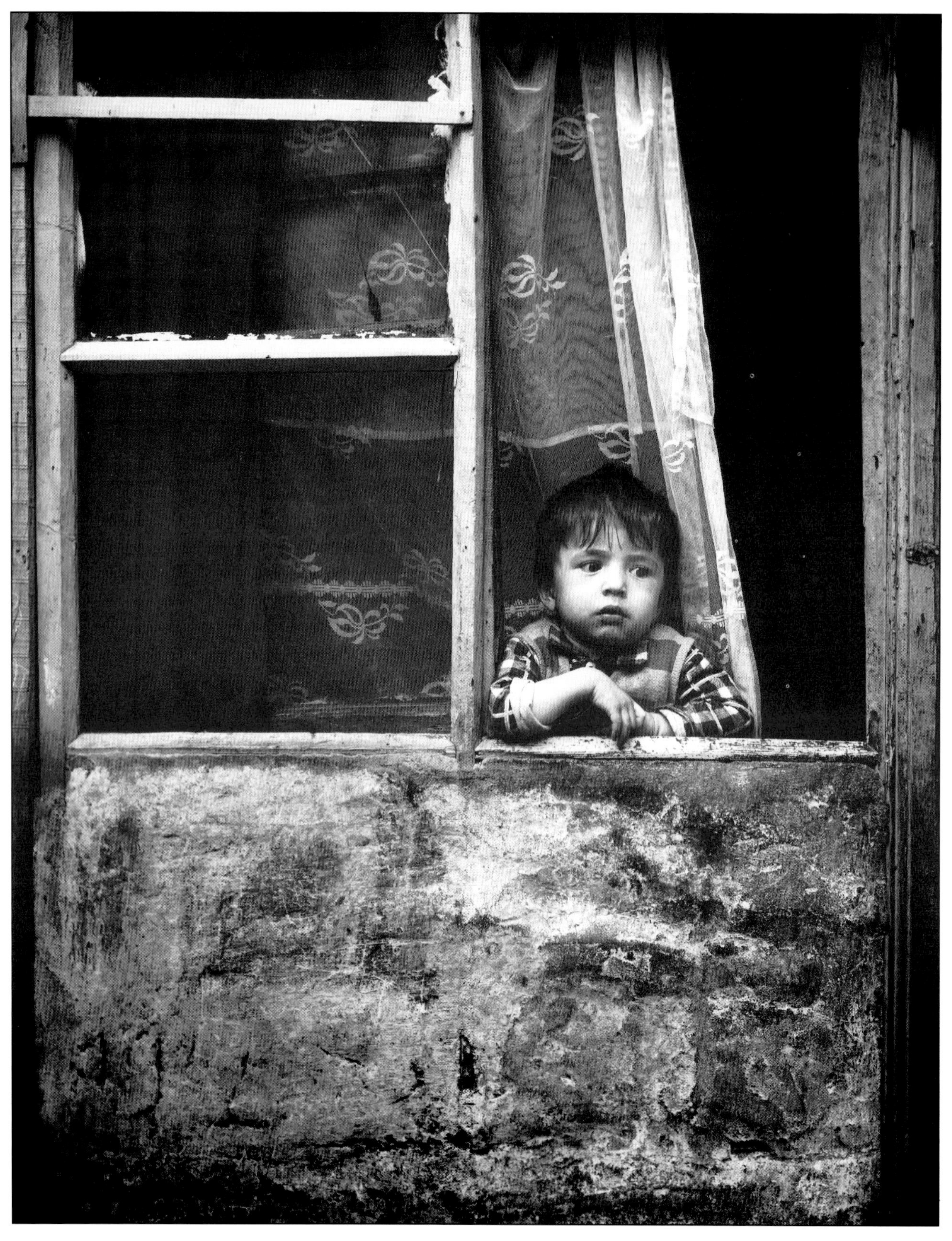

Child at window
Backstreets of Istanbul, Turkey

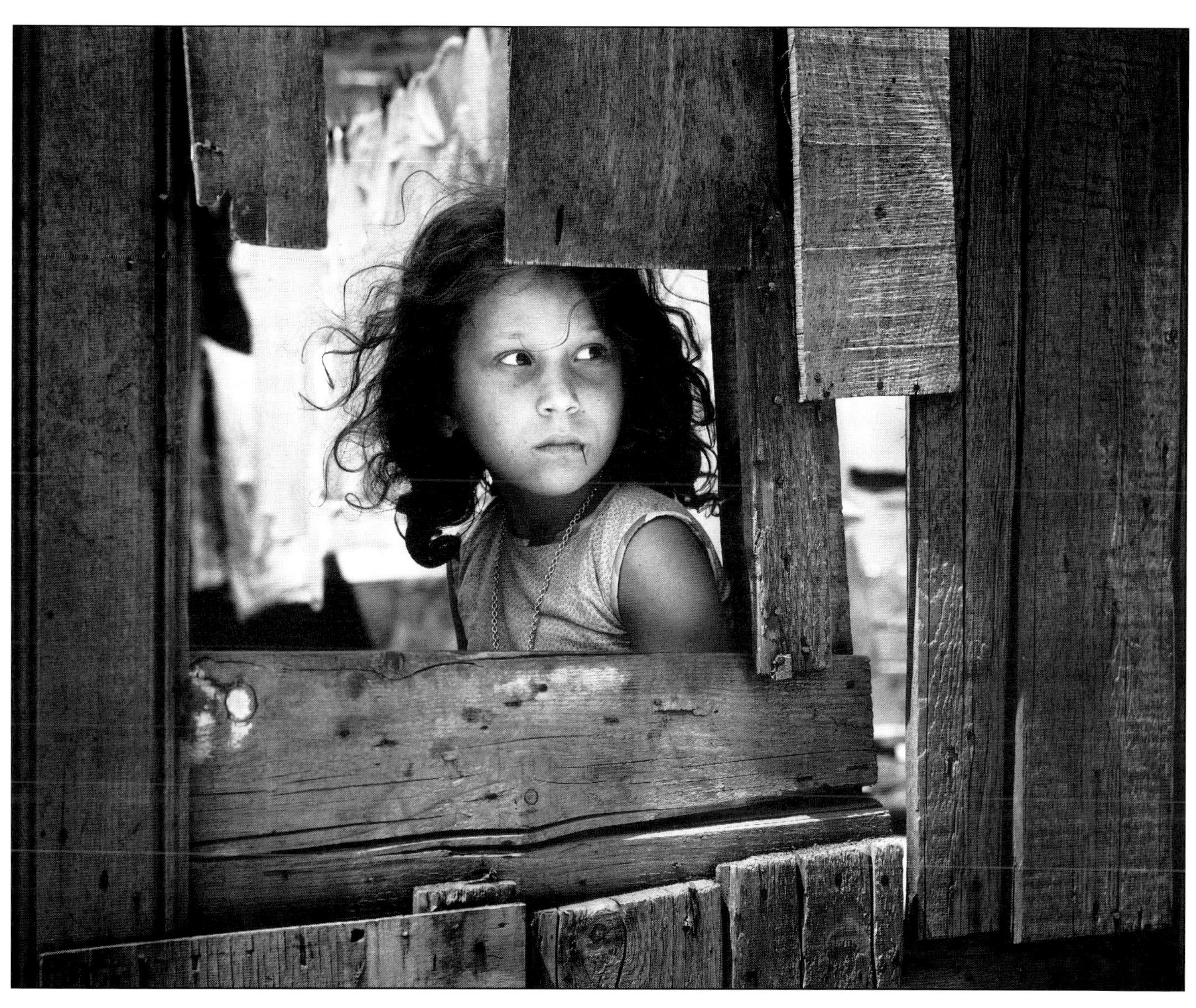

Child of Istanbul
Turkey

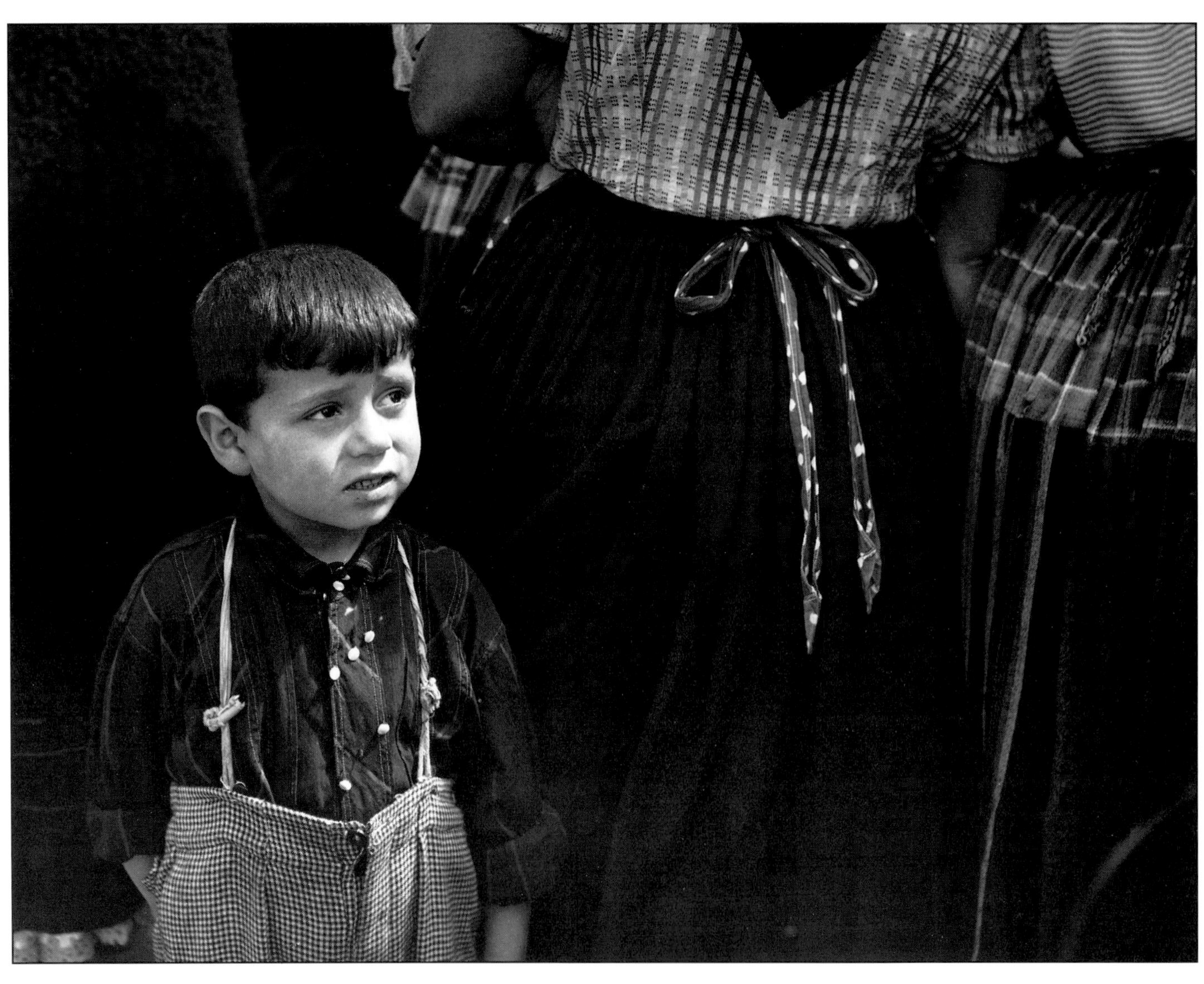

Boy with fishwives
Nazaré, Portugal

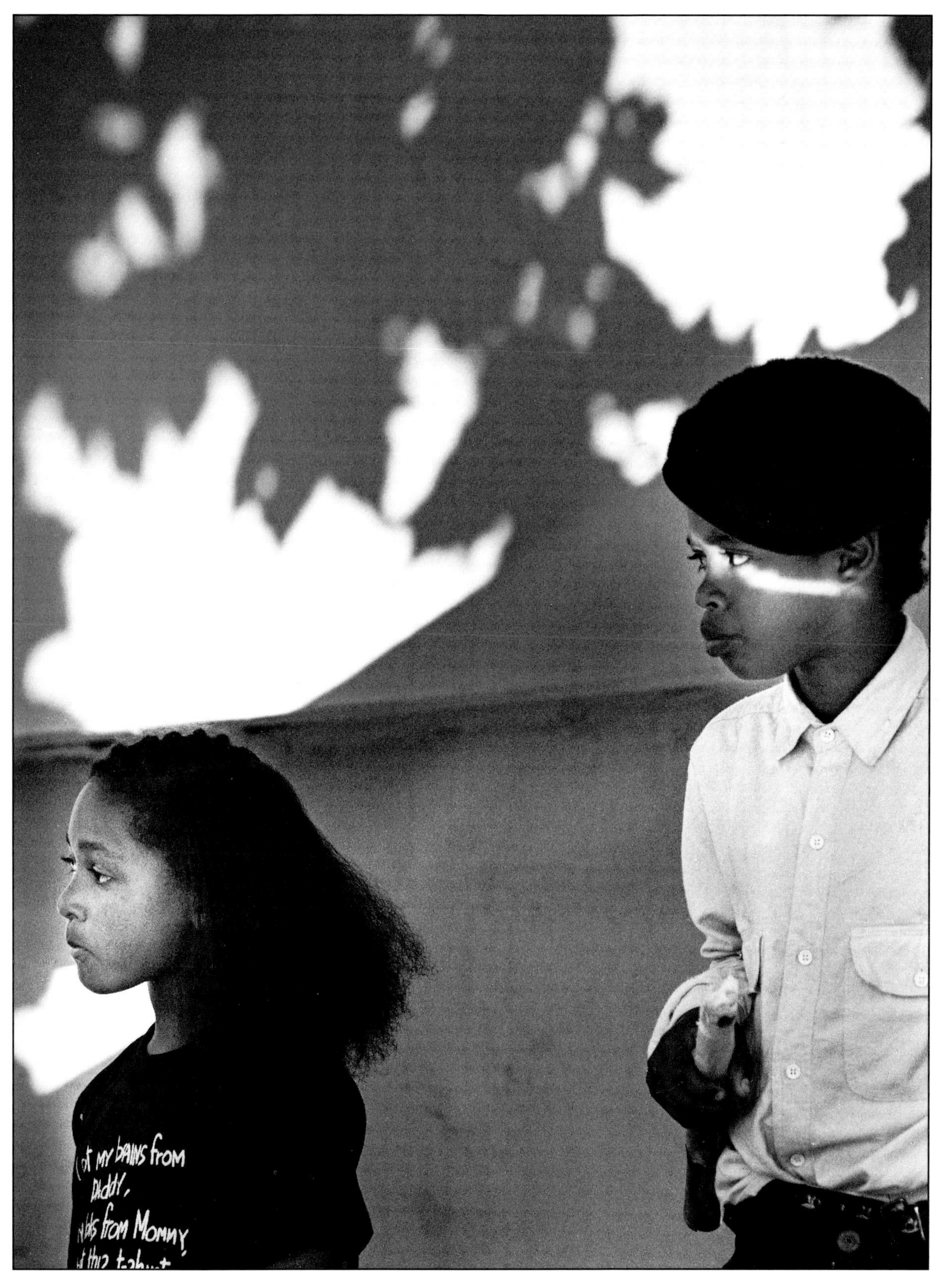

In the shadows
Notting Hill carnival, London

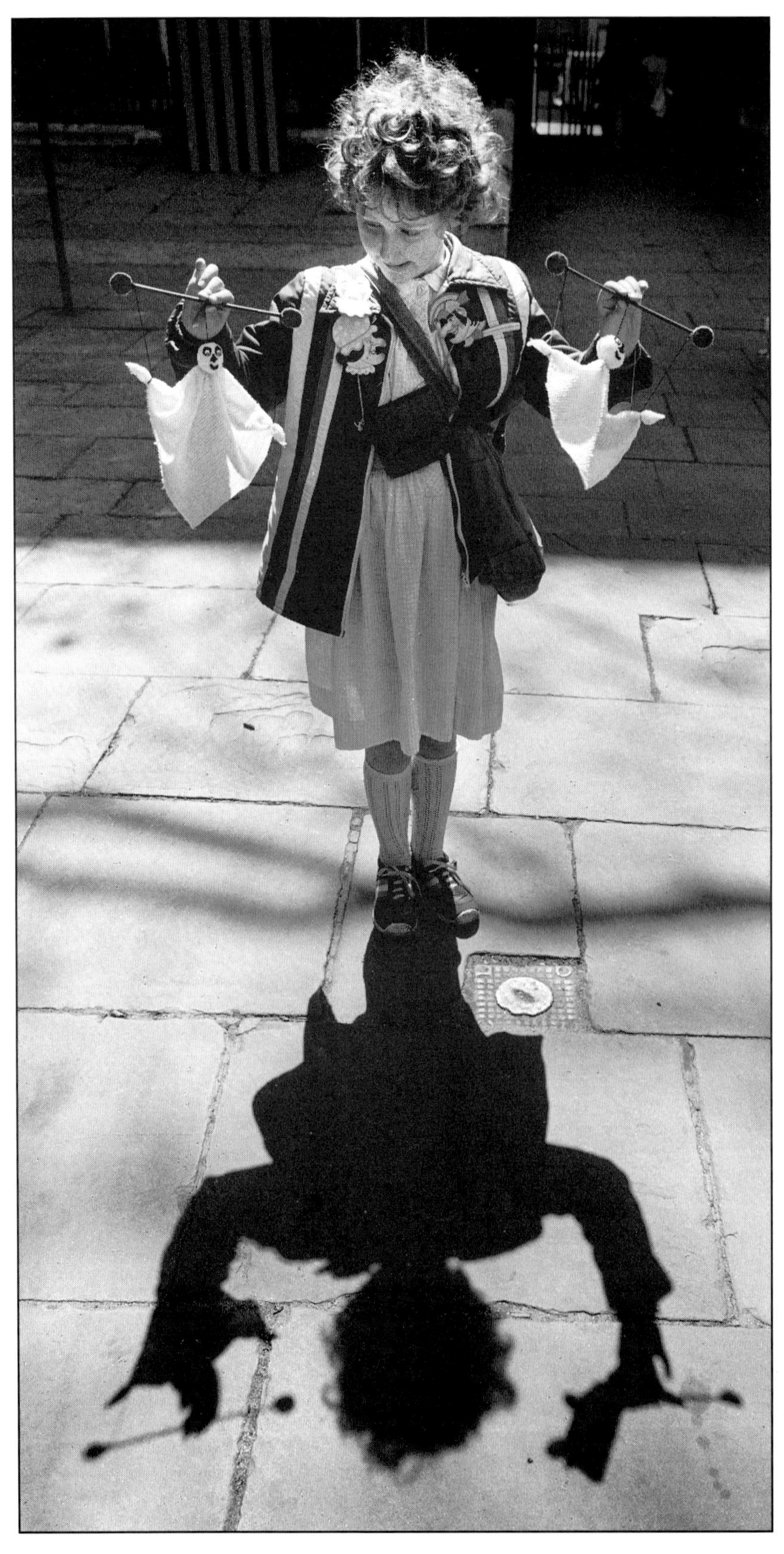

Shadow puppets
Covent Garden spring fair, London

I have a little shadow that goes in and out with me,
And what can be the use of him is more than I can see.
He is very, very like me from the heels up to the head;
And I see him jump before me, when I jump into my bed.

from My Shadow,
Robert Louis Stevenson

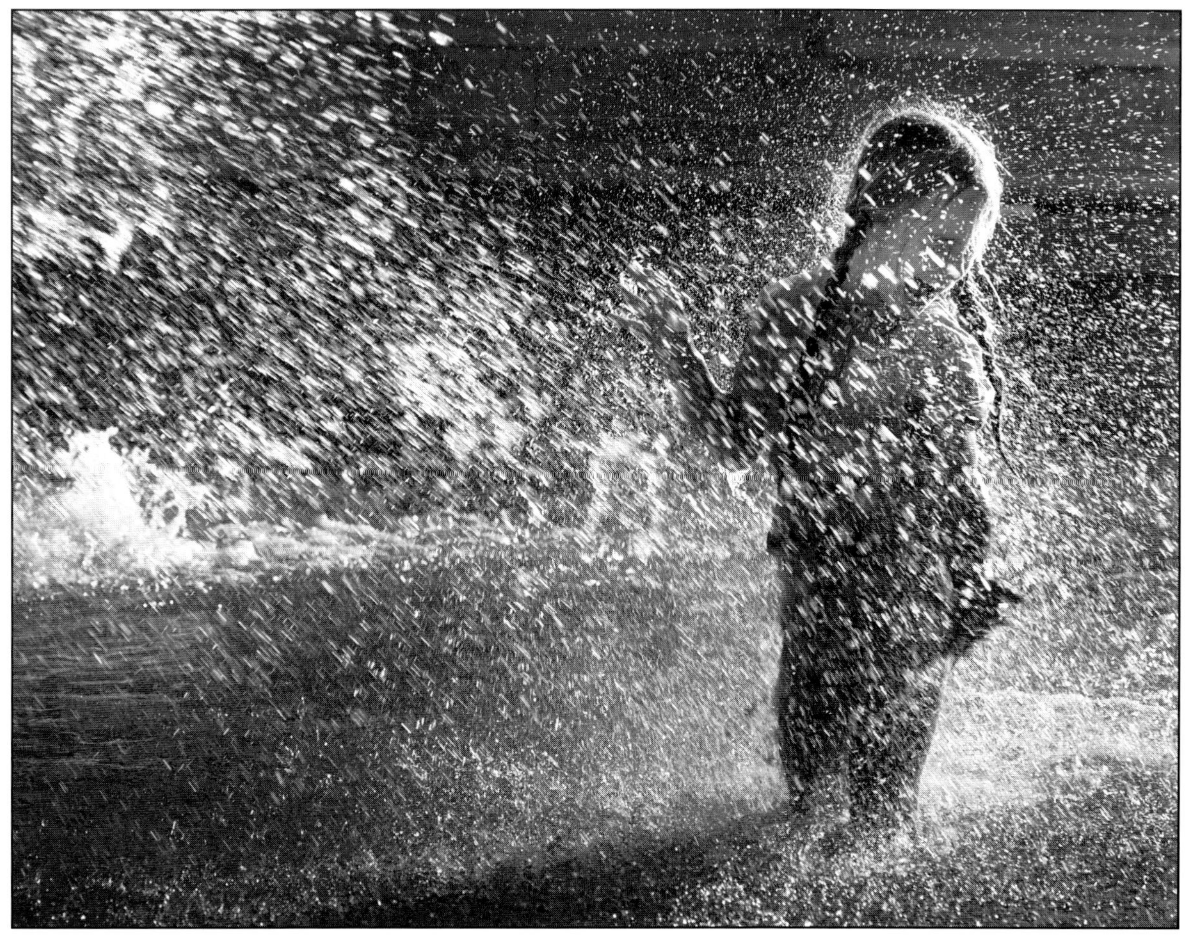

Splashed
Trafalgar Square, London

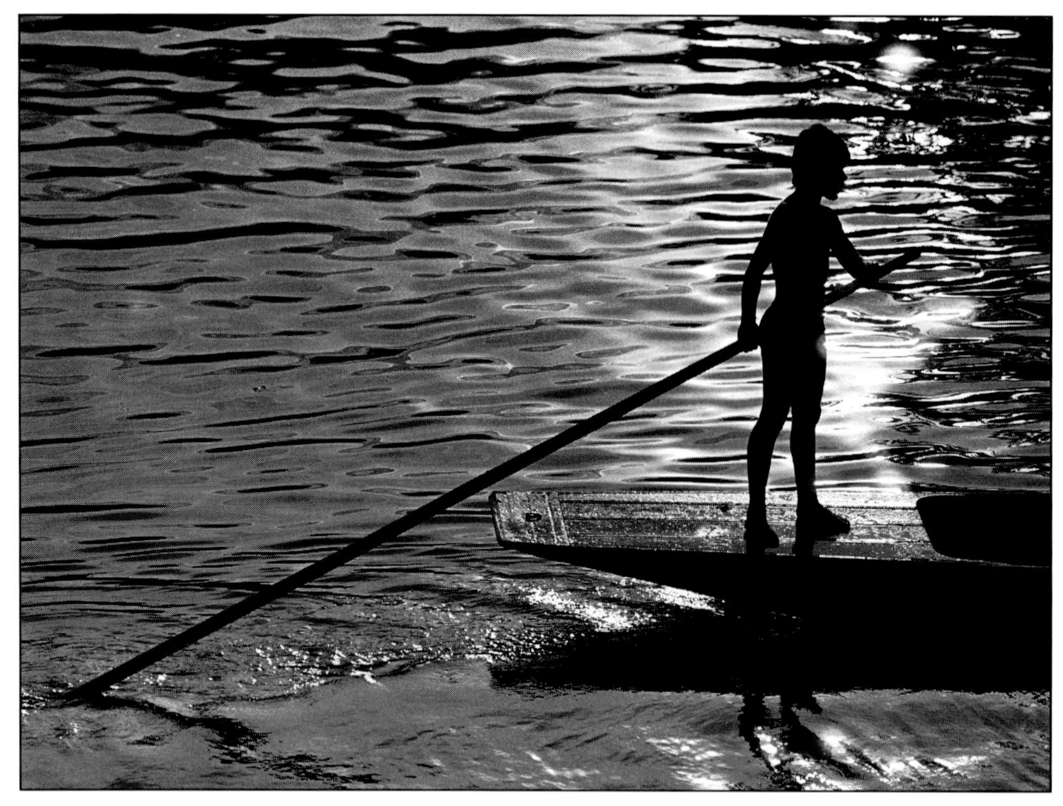

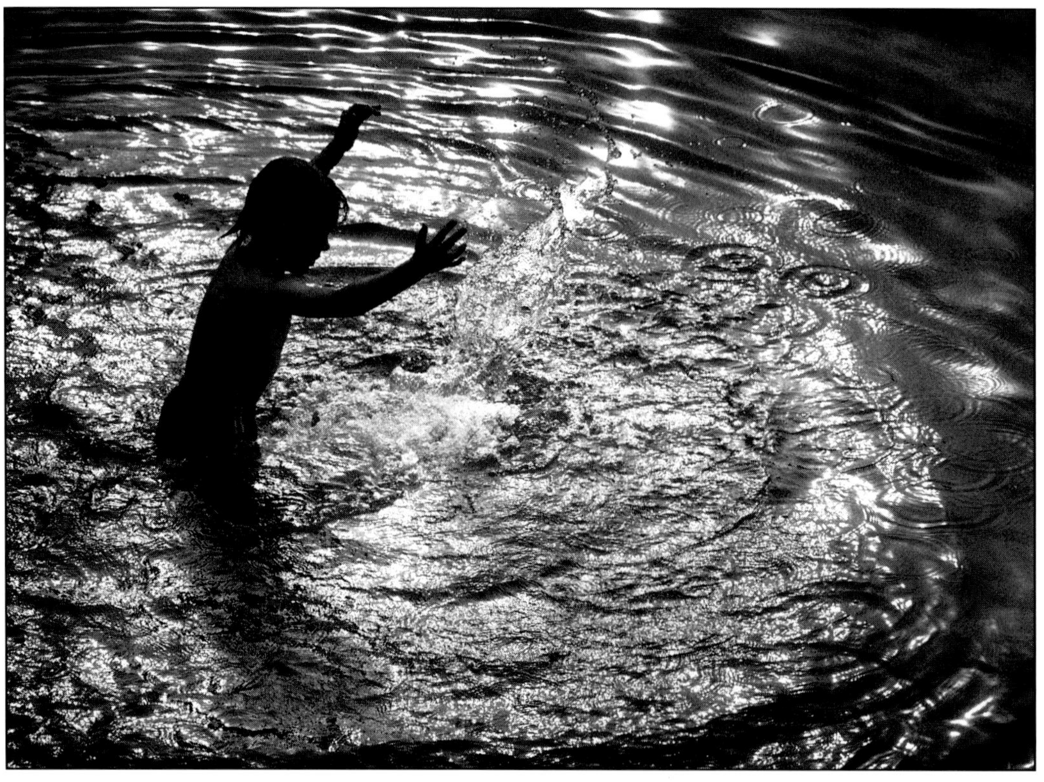

(top) **Punter,** River Thames at Oxford
(below) **Splashing about in the river,** Oxford

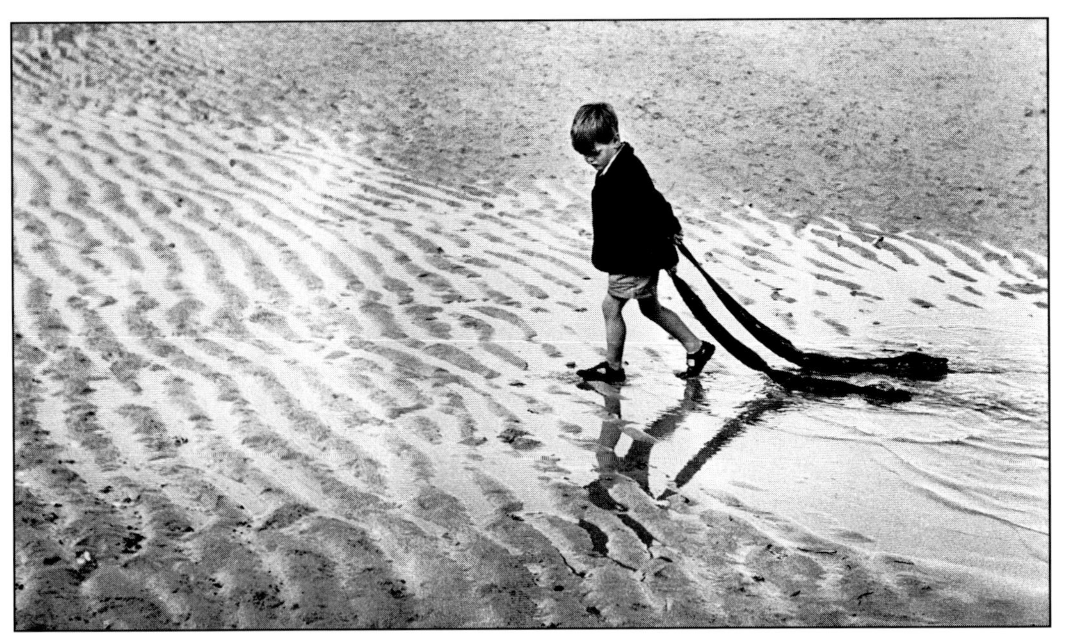

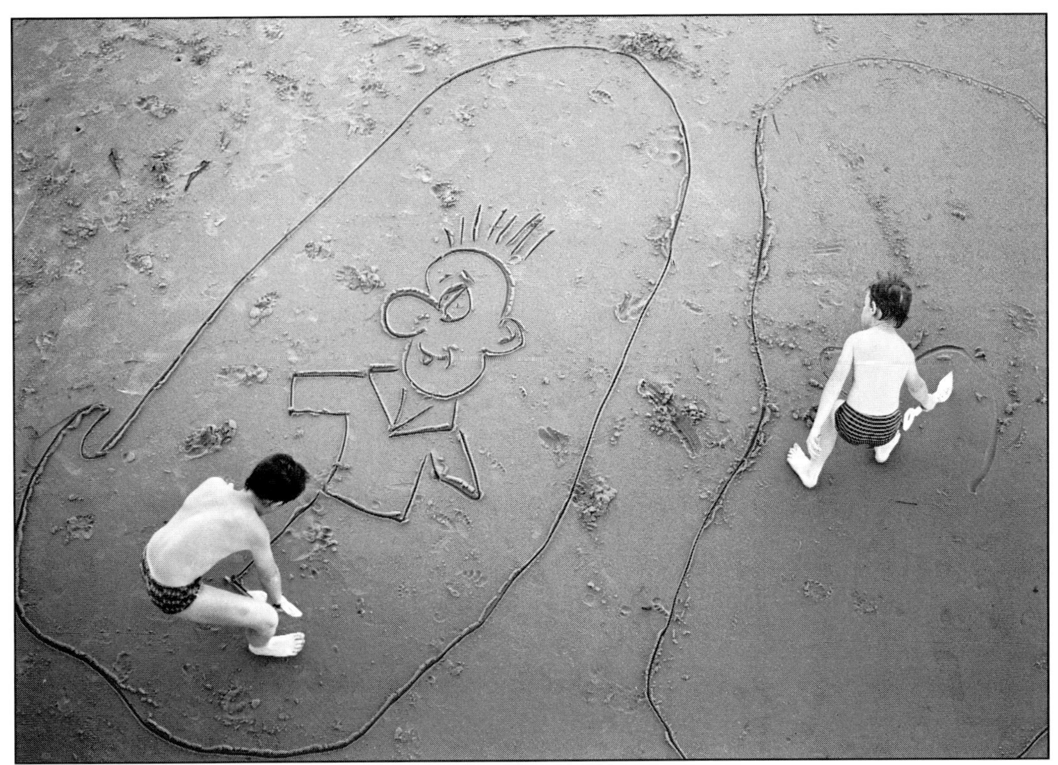

(top) *"I'll take them home"* (two dead fish)
(below) **Drawing in the sand,** *Bournemouth*

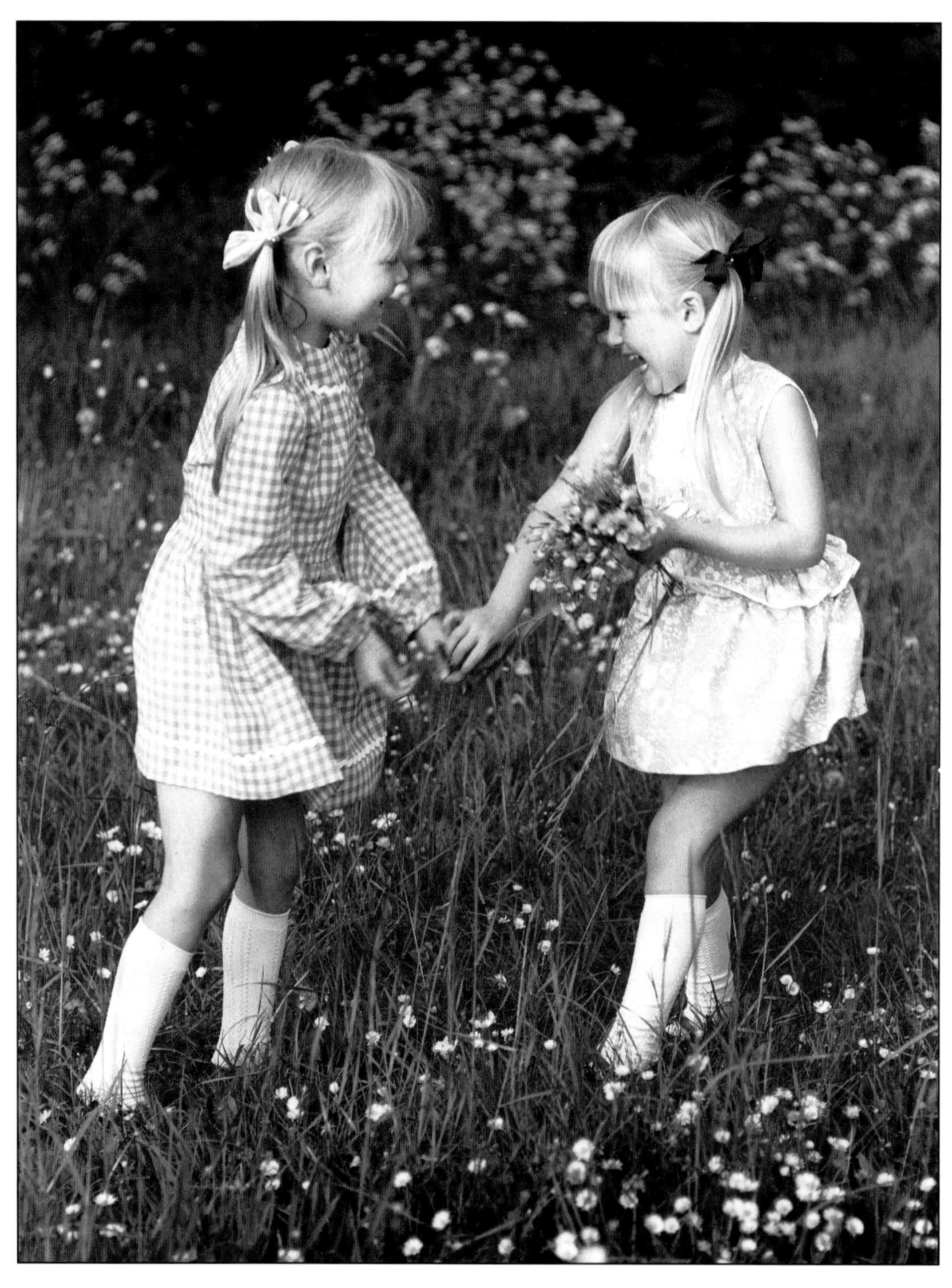

Sisters playing
Bracknell, Berkshire

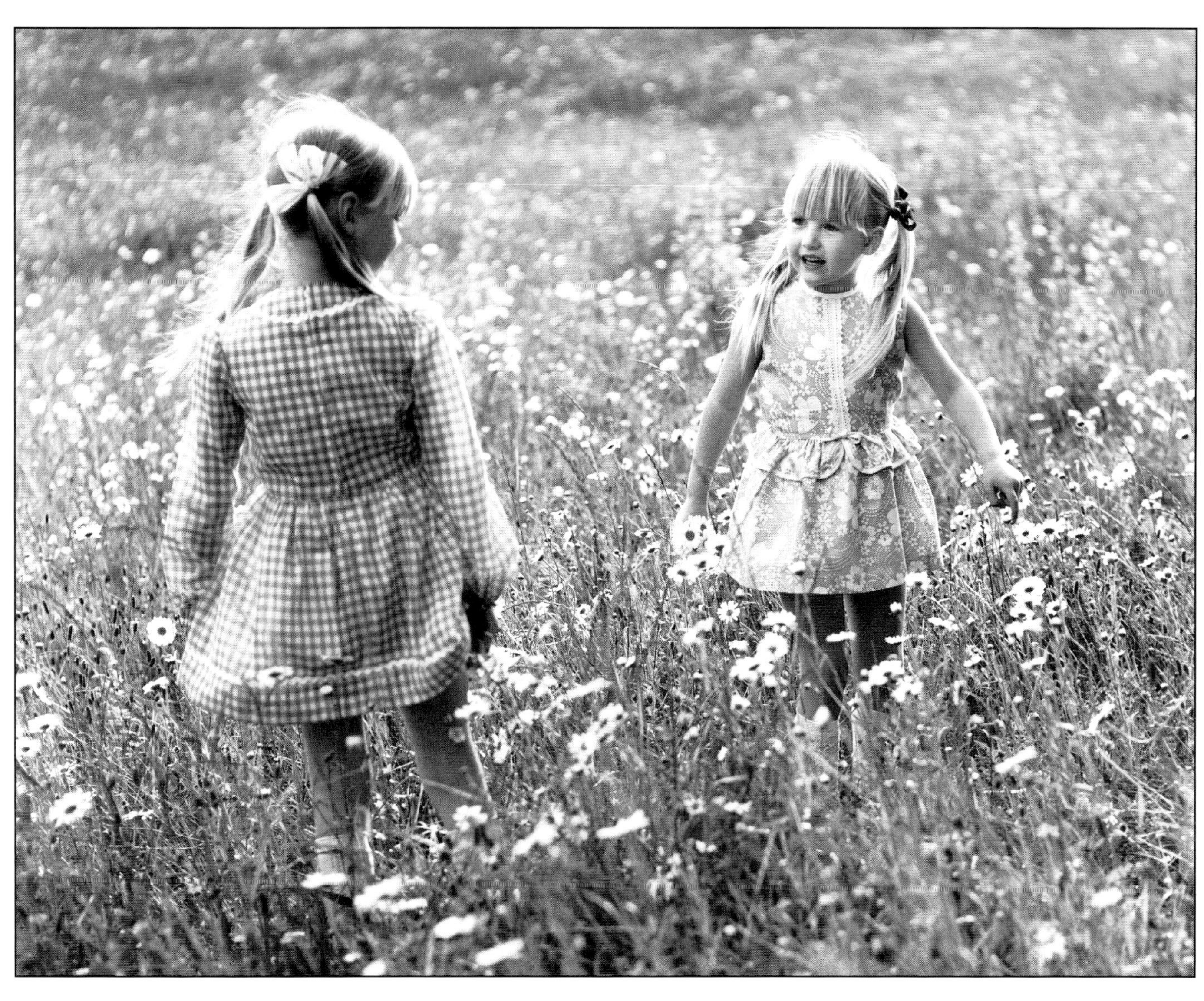

Amongst the daisies
Bracknell, Berkshire

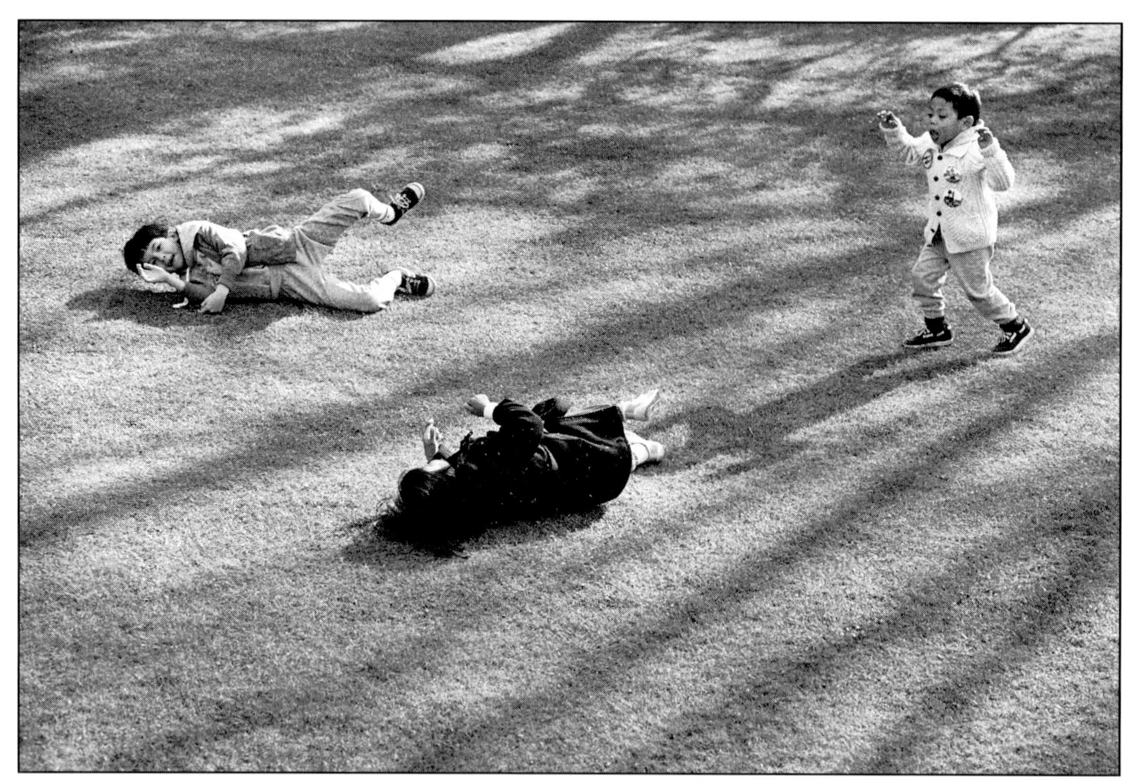

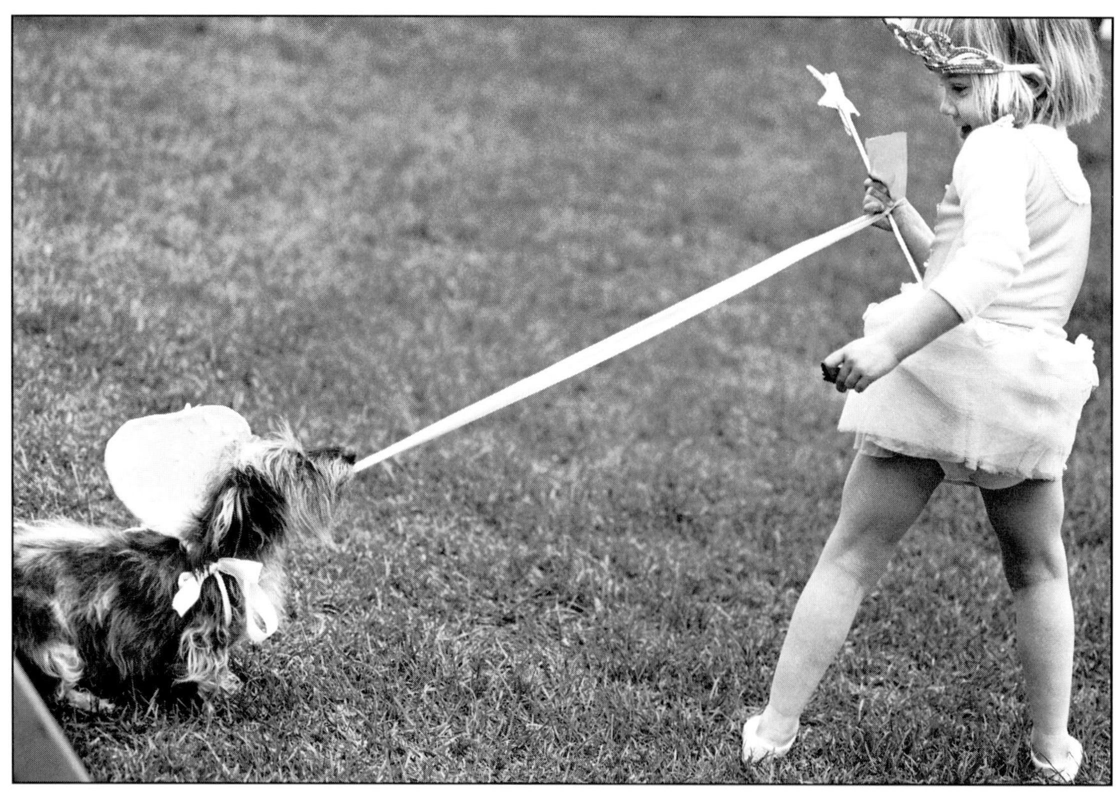

(top) **Fooling around in the park,** *near Little Venice, London*
(below) ***A very reluctant exhibit,*** *Spring Fair dog show, Richmond, Surrey*

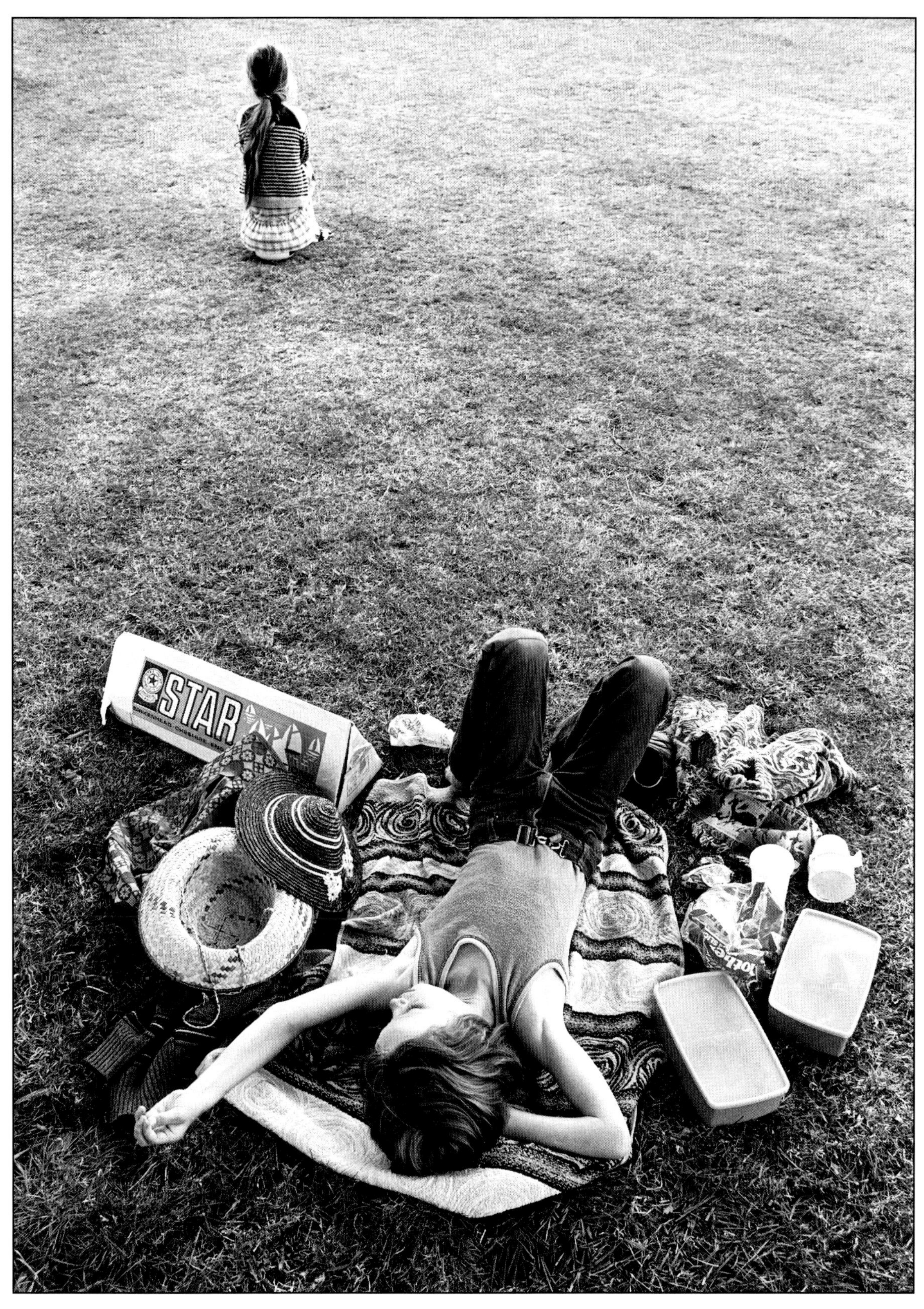

Summer tiff interrupts play
London

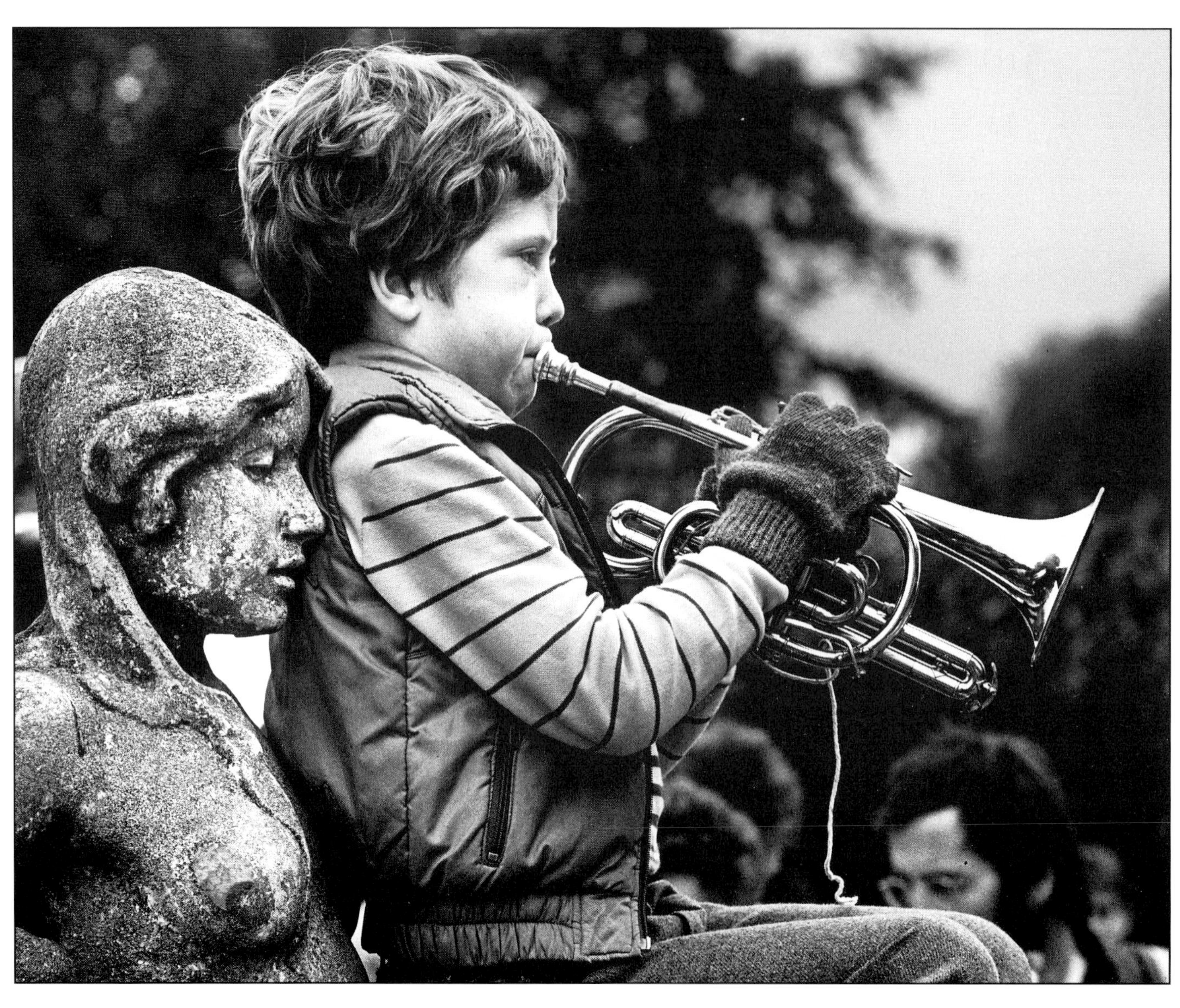

Jazz trumpeter with angel
Hyde Park, London

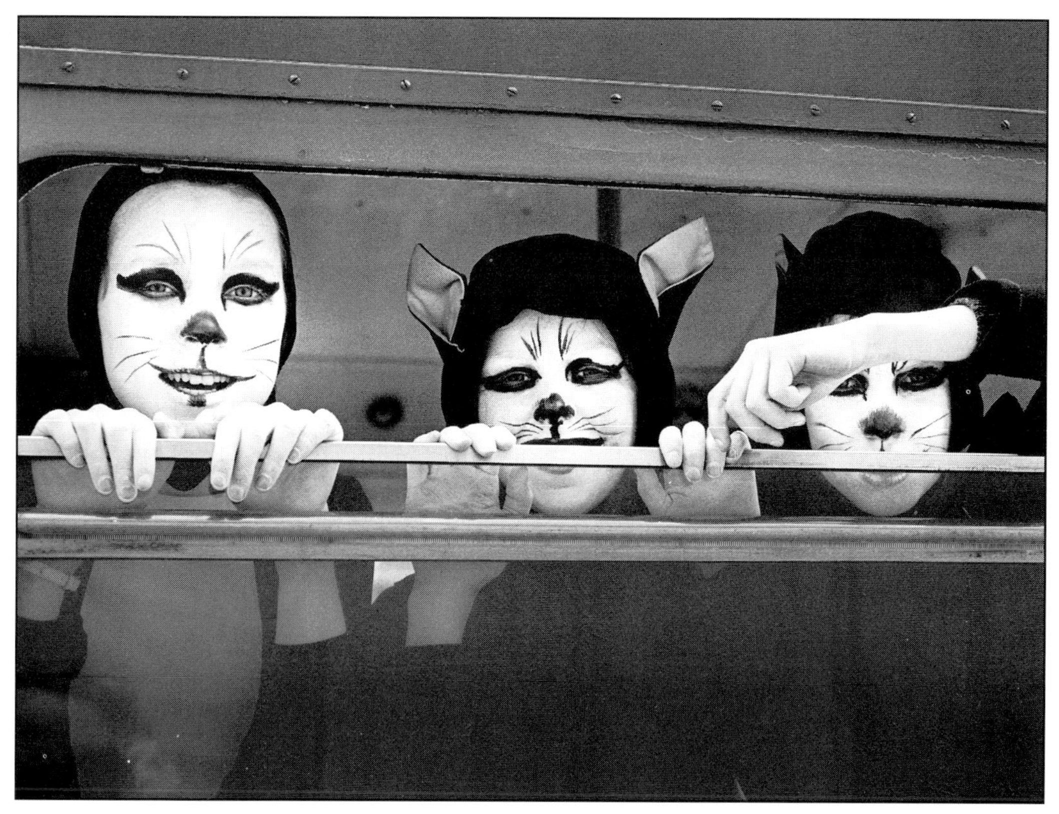

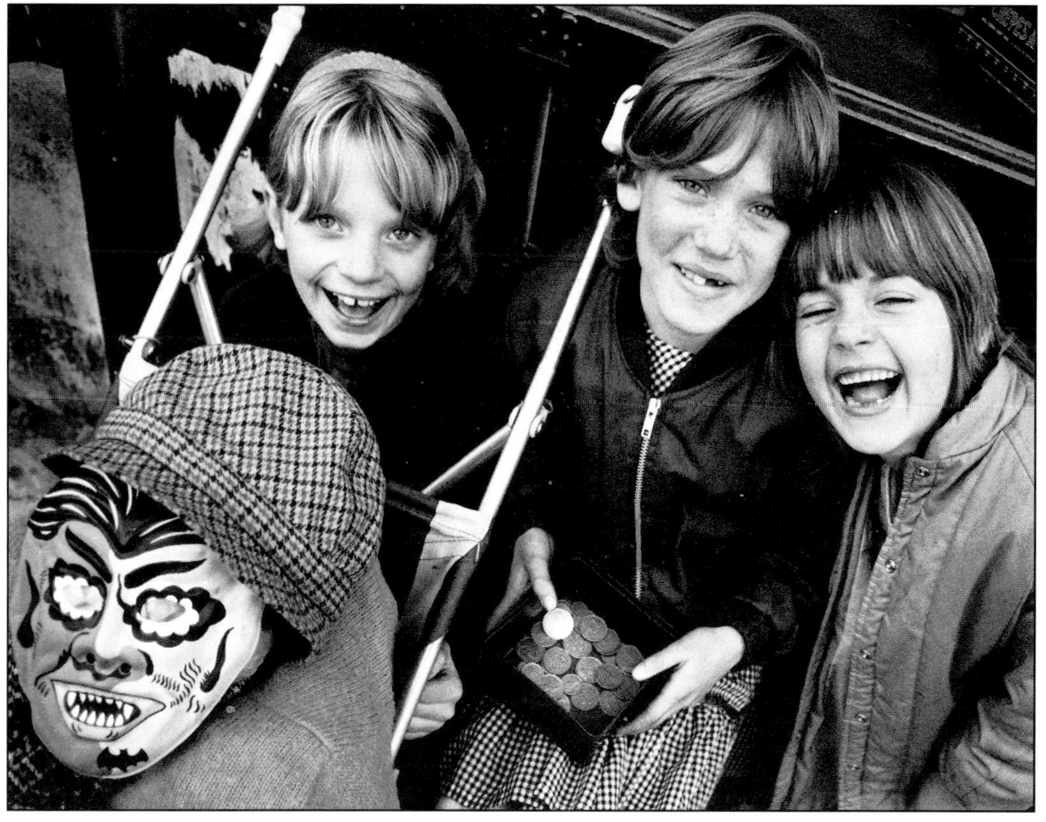

(top) **Three miaows,** Cat parade, Ieper, Belgium
(below) **Guy and girls,** Blackheath, London

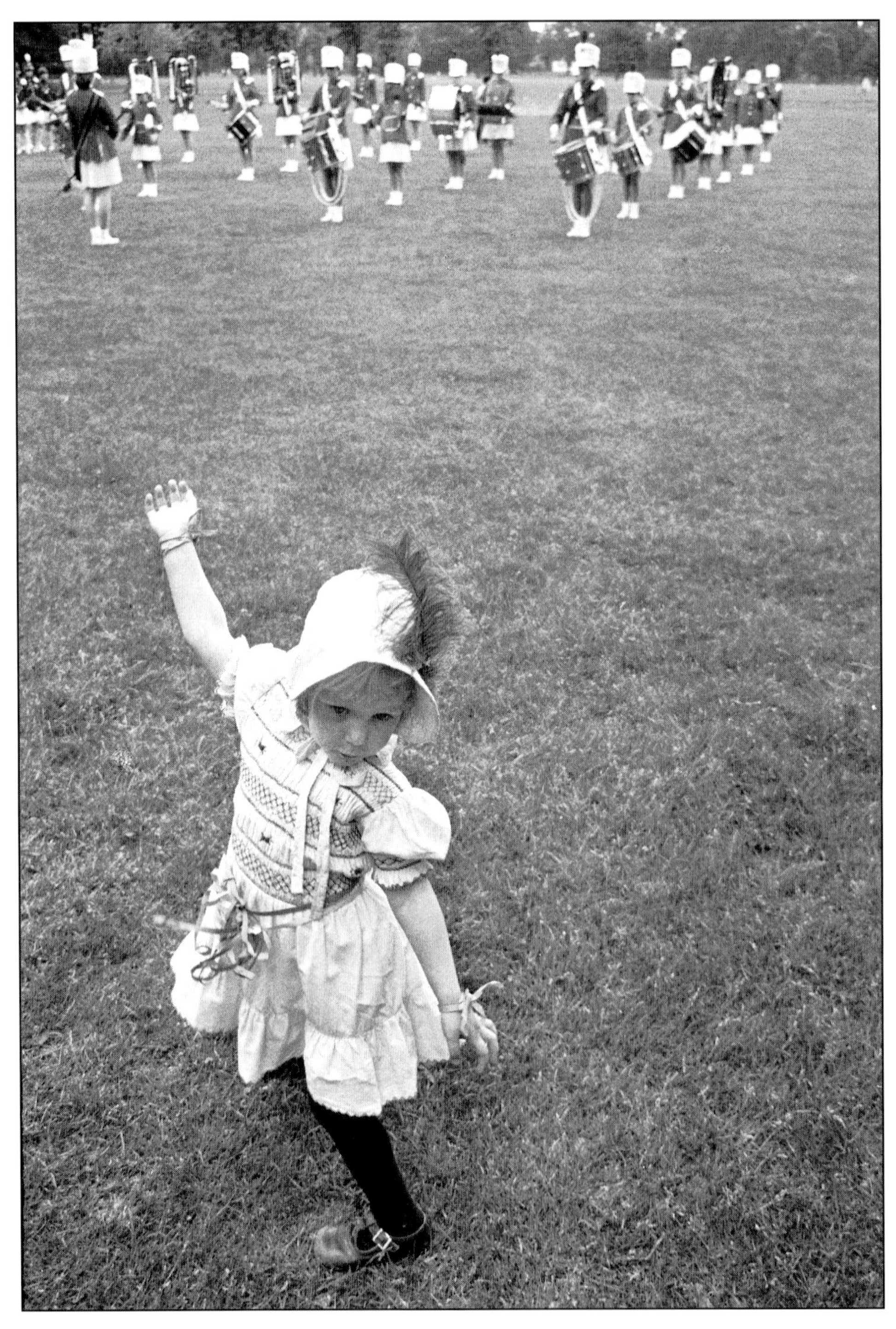

Dancing to her own tune
London

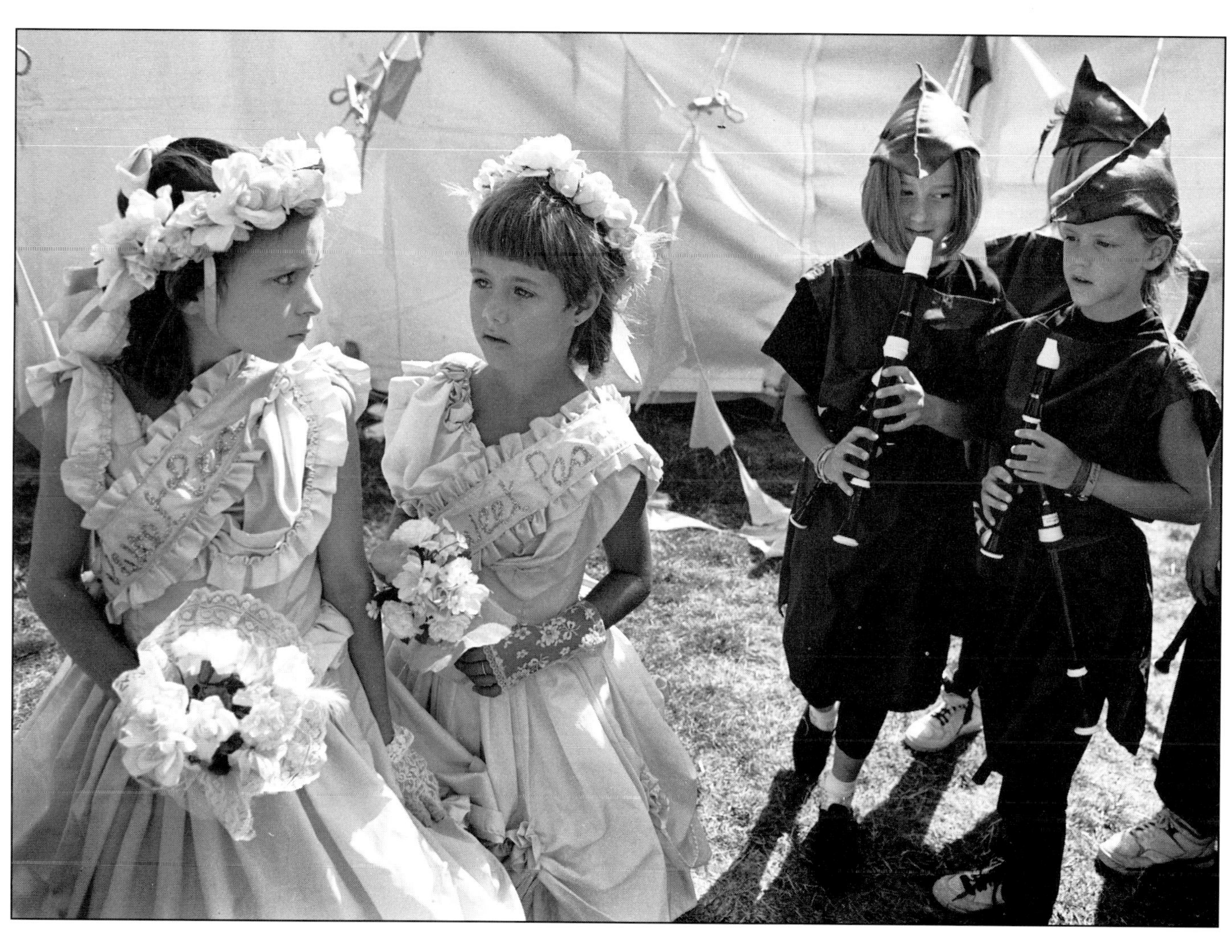

Sweet peas
Hampton Court craft fair

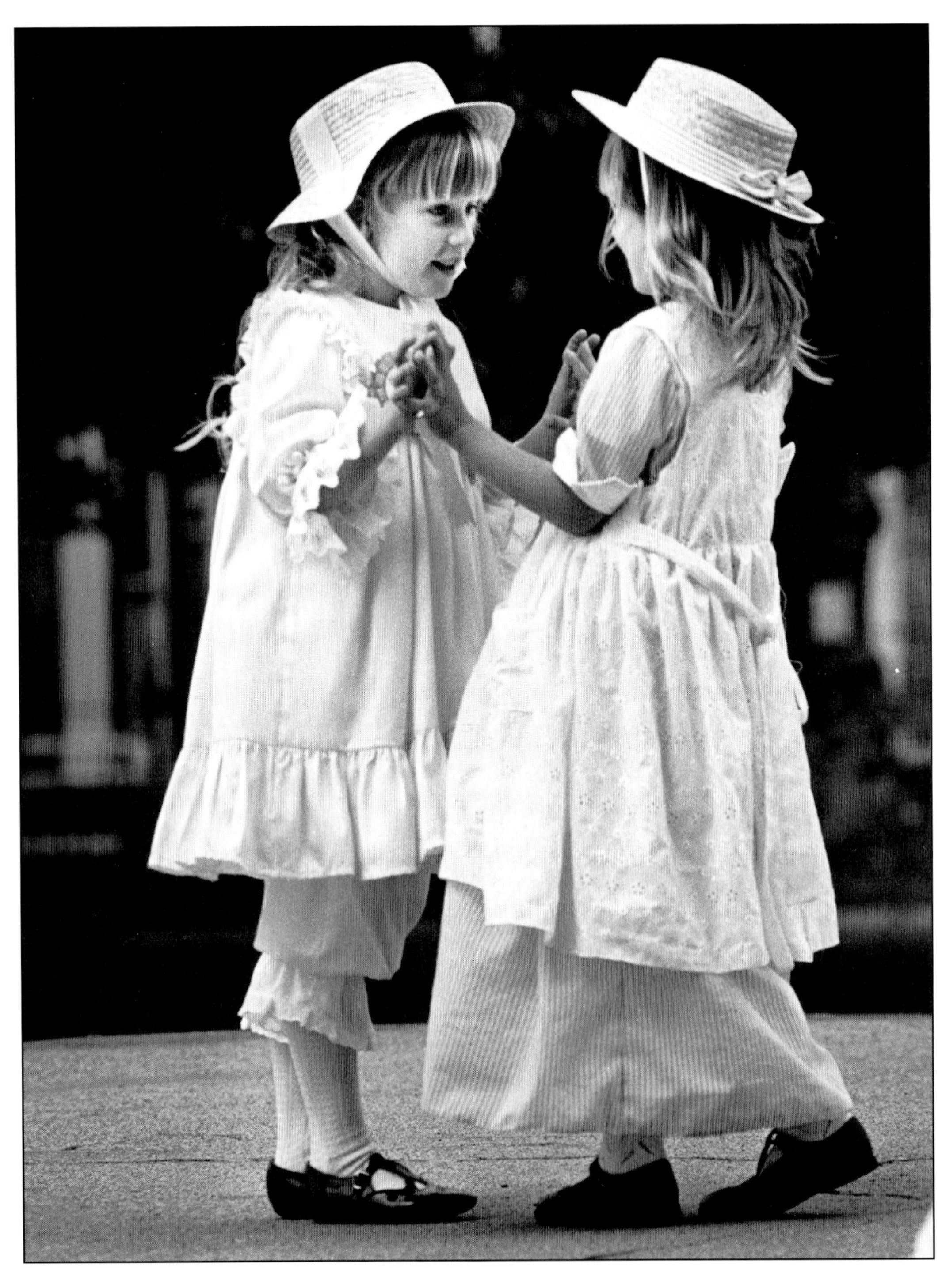

Touching game
Dickens festival, Rochester, Kent

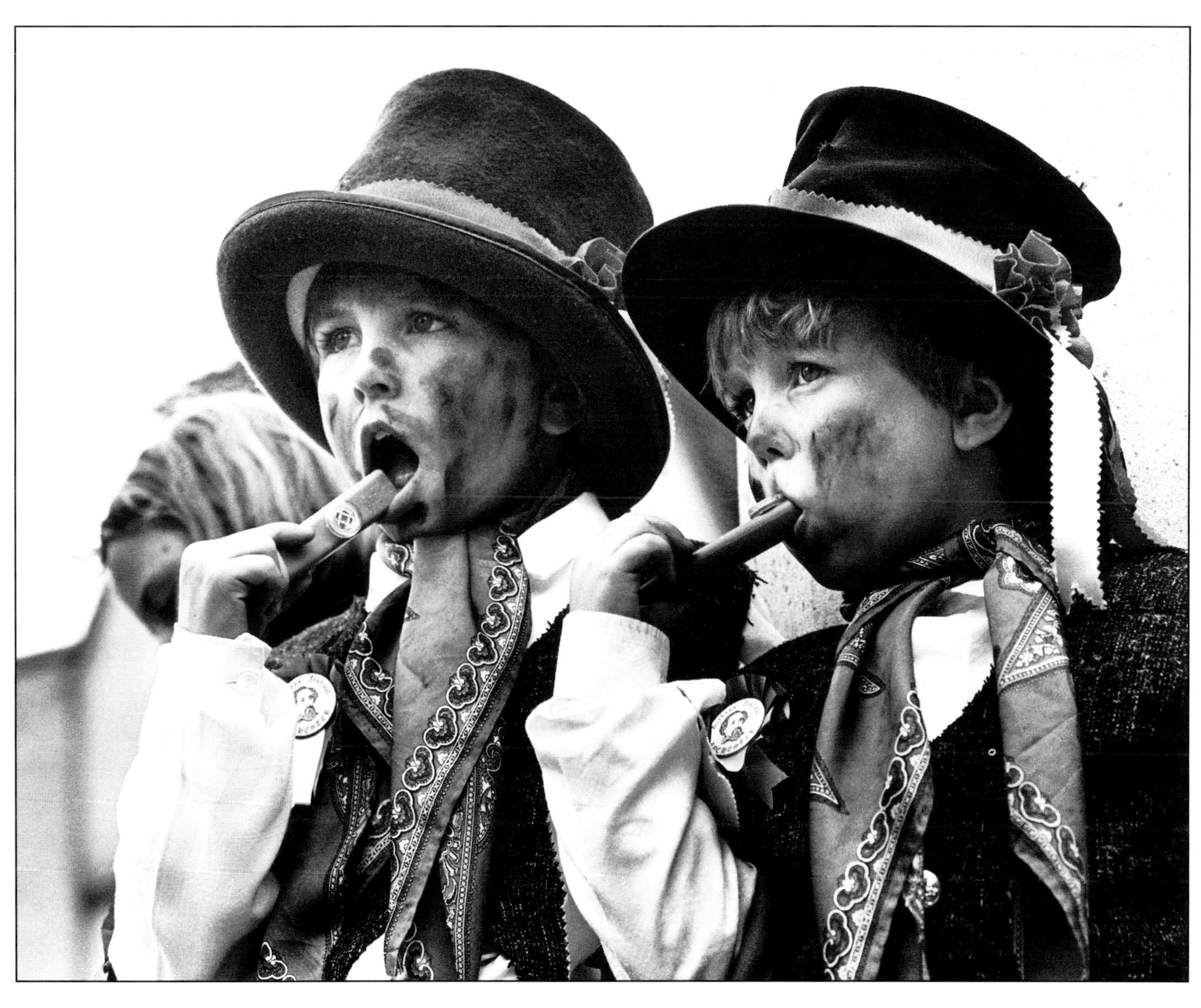

The toffs
The sweeps festival, Rochester, Kent

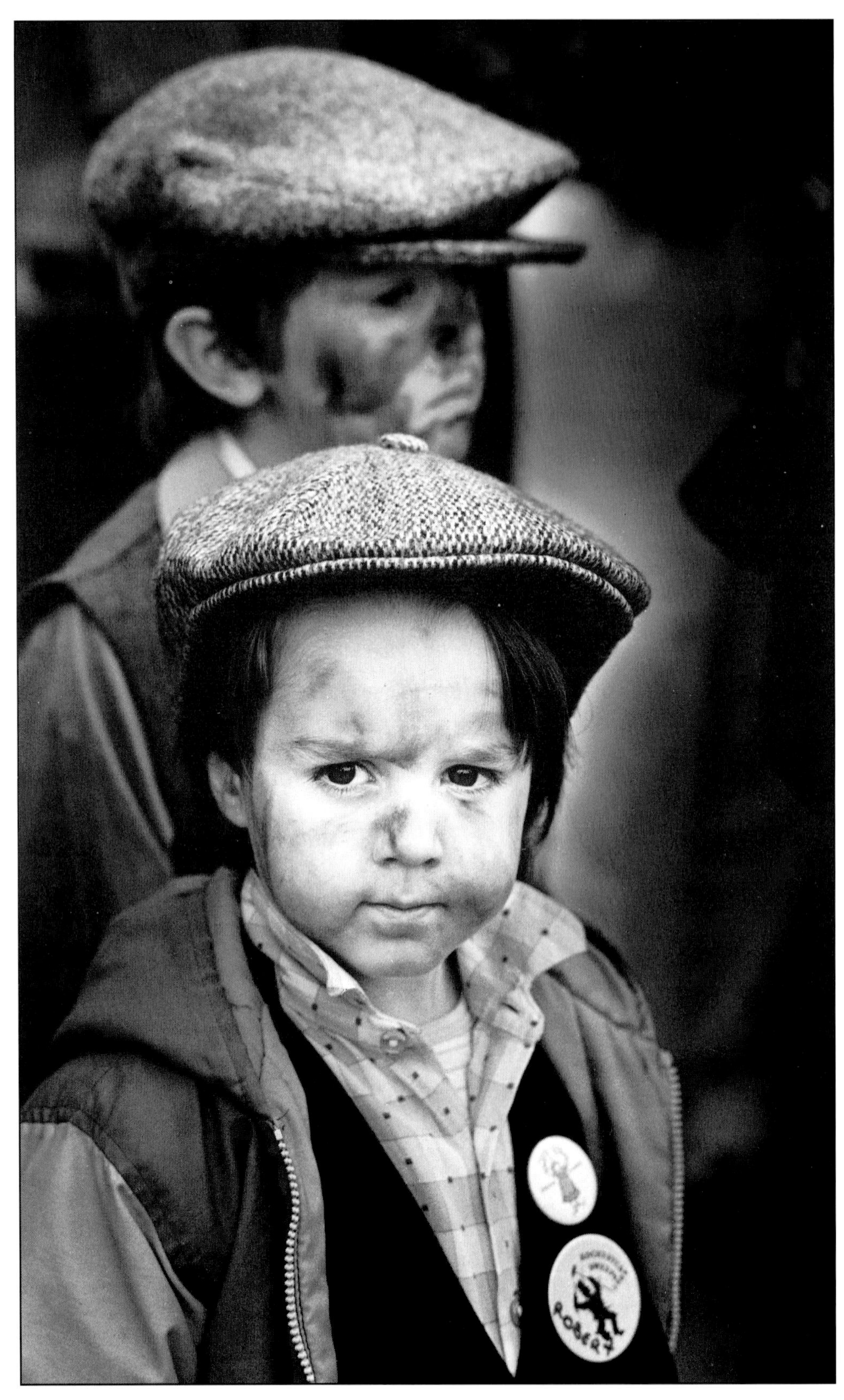

Flat caps
Sweeps festival, Rochester, Kent

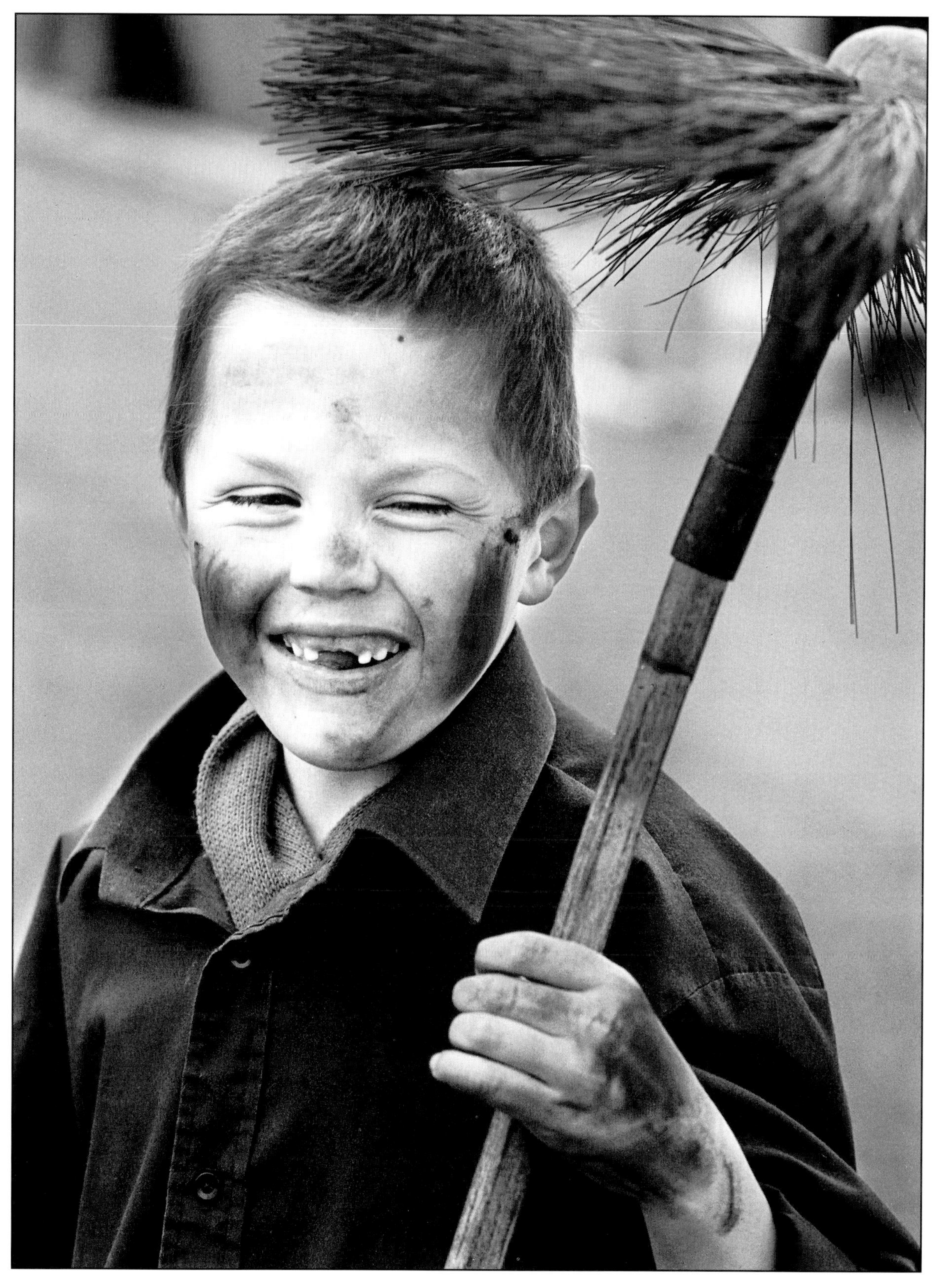

Toothless grin
Annual sweeps festival, Rochester, Kent

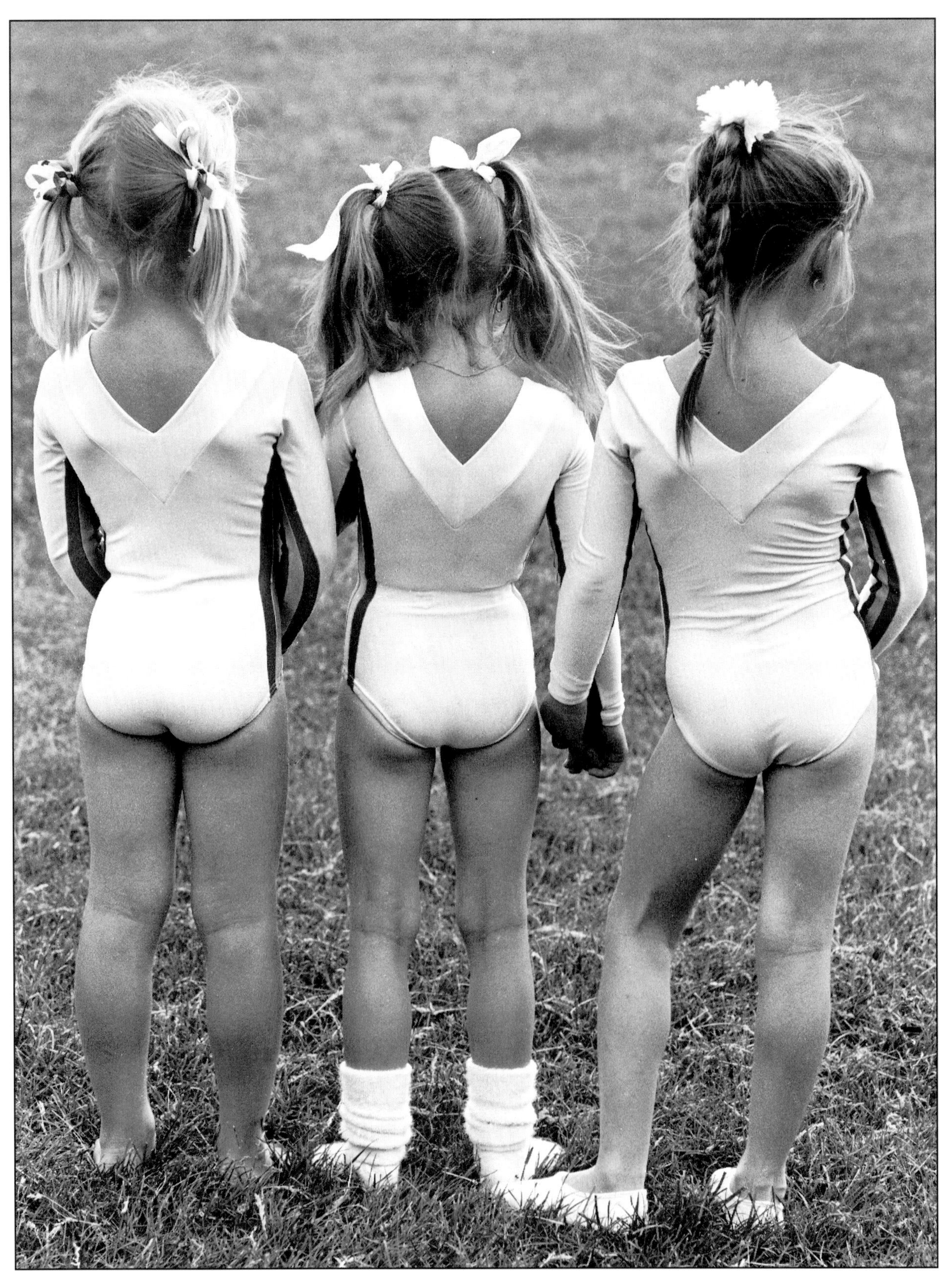

Three full backs
Gymnastic display, London

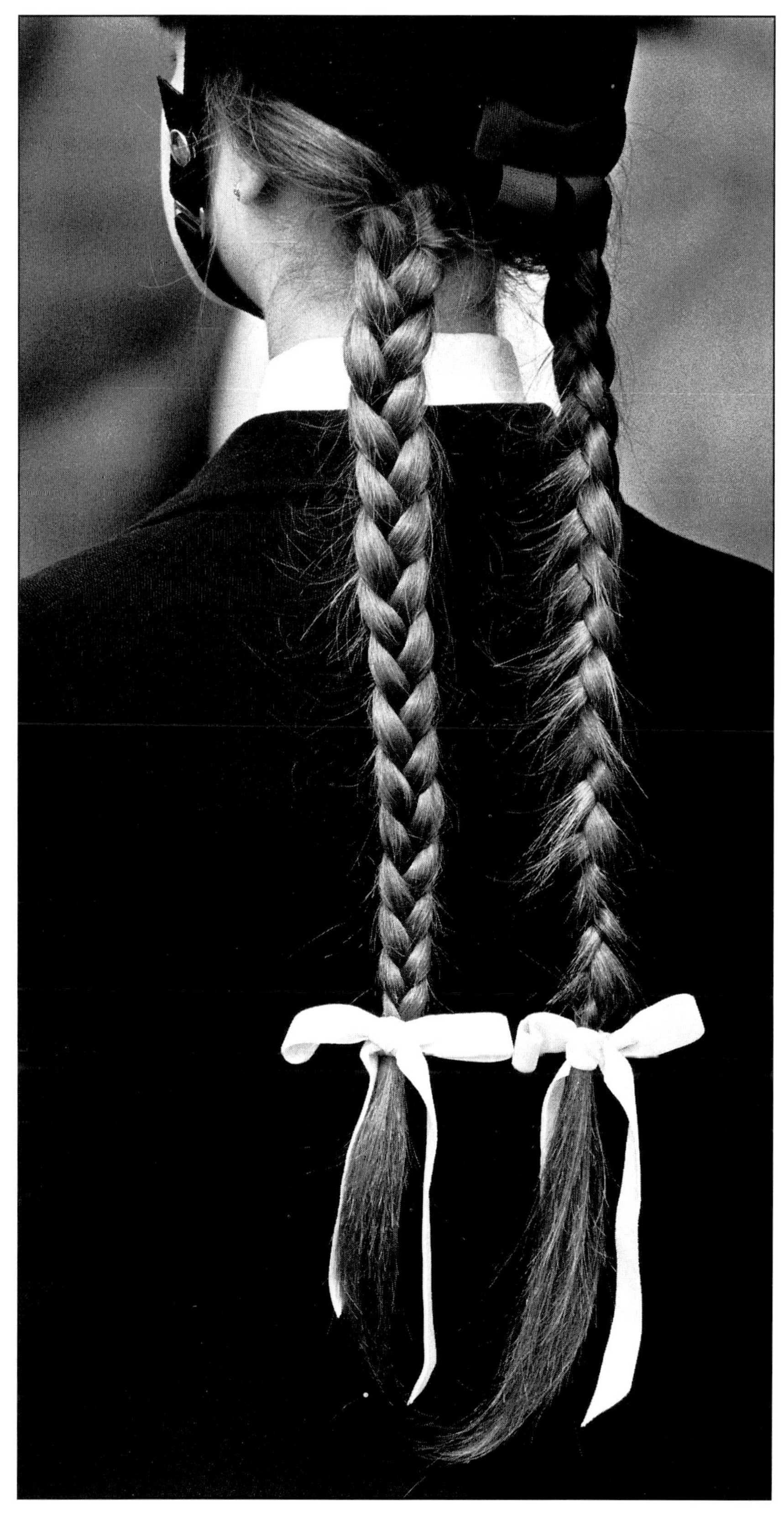

Plaits
Gymkhana, Hyde Park, London

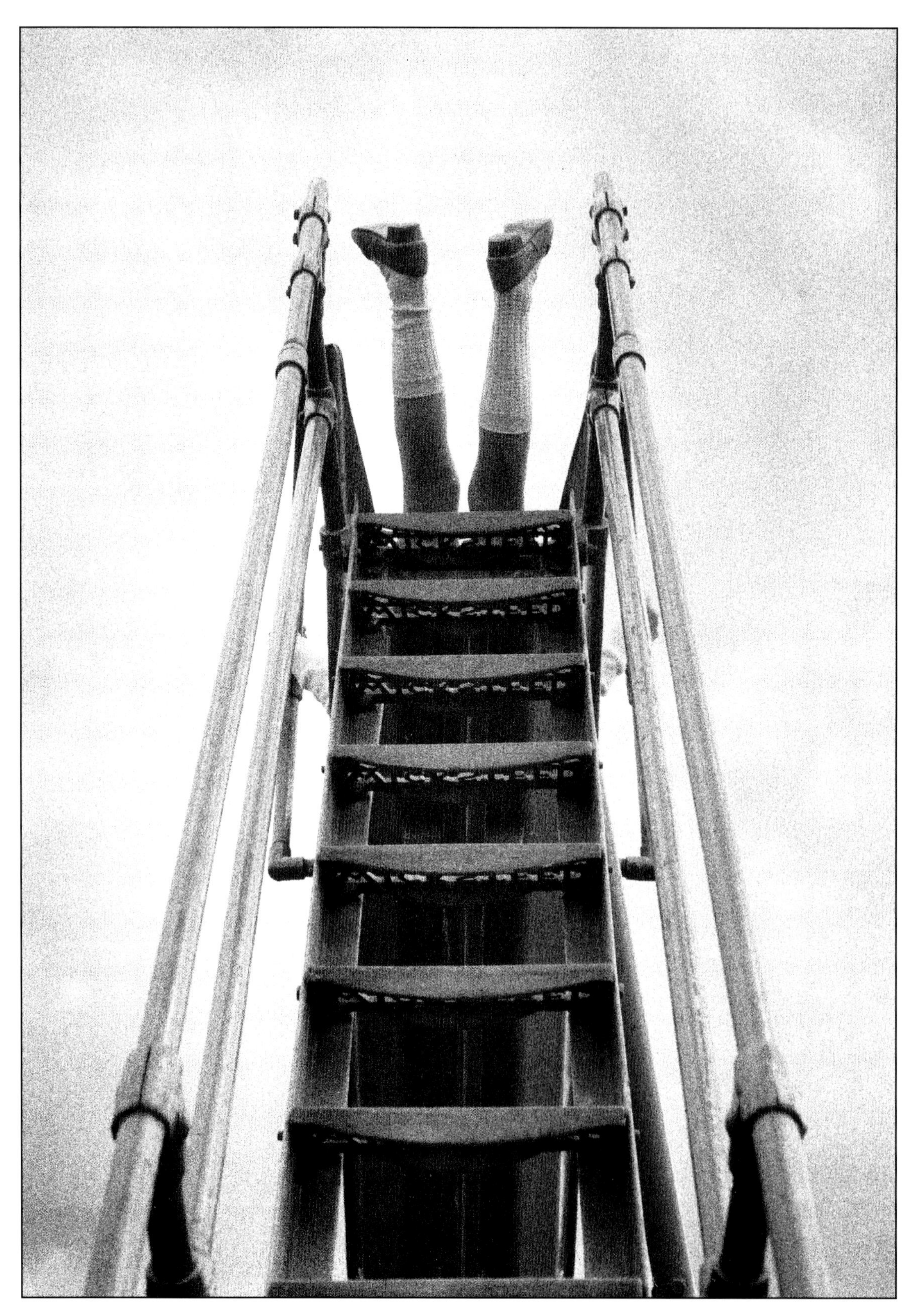

At the top of the slide
Bracknell, Berkshire

TO ANY READER

As from the house your Mother sees
You playing round the garden trees,
So you may see, if you will look
Through the windows of this book,
Another child, far, far away,
And in another garden, play.
But do not think you can at all,
By knocking on the window, call
That child to hear you. He intent
Is all on his play-business bent.
He does not hear; he will not look,
Nor yet be lured out of his book.
For, long ago, the truth to say,
He has grown up and gone away,
And it is but a child of air
That lingers in the garden there.

Robert Louis Stevenson

Technical aspects

If you check back in the pages of annuals like the *Photography Year Book* or *Photograms* in the 1950s, you will find that the majority of photographs in that period were taken with the combination of a 6x6cm twin lens reflex (usually a Rolleiflex) and Ilford's FP3 film. I was no exception: having started with an Ikoflex, I eventually progressed to owning the 'standard' medium format camera of the day and almost always loaded FP3.

I remained faithful to this combination for monochrome photography longer than most. Whilst the single lens reflex 35mm camera really took over in the 1960s, it was not until the end of the 1970s that I changed completely to 35mm for black and white work (although I had been using 35mm for colour slides from the outset).

It was my experience of the versatility of interchangeable lenses for colour work on my 35mm Olympus OM1, which finally persuaded me to forsake the larger negative size of the twin lens cameras, which I had usually only armed with standard focal length lenses. The transition to these horribly tiny negatives was not without its problems and frustrations initially.

The turning point was my good fortune in winning a Vivitar VI enlarger as part of the 'Master Photographer of the Year' prize in the original *Photo Technique* magazine competition. It had an excellent 50mm f/2.8 lens and a glassless negative carrier that really seemed to keep the negative flat. I have learnt recently that in winning this competition, I just pipped a promising young photographer who is now editor of Britain's best selling monthly photo magazine. William Cheung subsequently bought a Vivitar VI (unfortunately no longer manufactured) and, like me, still uses it to this day.

Then, in 1980, Ilford introduced XP1-400 film. I soon settled down with this film, rating it at EI 250, knowing that I had a little extra speed in hand when lighting conditions deteriorated. I have stayed with this film and its replacement XP2, processing it (until its demise) in the dedicated Ilford chemistry for 8 minutes at 32°C.

Obviously, I have used a great variety of printing papers over the years, starting (as I recall) with Ilford's Plastica. My first 20x16" exhibition prints, in about 1957, were made on what I believe was Ilford's first multigrade paper. I soon changed to graded papers, eventually settling almost completely for Ilford's Galerie, which I used for all my exhibition prints for several years.

More recently, I changed to Ilford's fibre-based Multigrade, which for the present is my preferred paper for exhibition work. Its most obvious advantage is that it allows me to stock one packet of paper instead of three. But the even greater advantage is the fine-tuning of grades, which extends to being able to use more than one level of filtration within the same print.

There is nothing intricate in my print processing techniques: two to three minutes in the developer, a quick slosh through water, and then a Hypam fixer. I do take care with the washing: twelve changes of water over a period of up to two hours, before drying face up on a four-tier nylon gauze rack. Not exactly standard textbook archival permanence stuff, but (in my experience) effective, as my earliest prints are now 30 years old.

It was only last year that I discovered the use of selenium toner to enrich the blacks in Multigrade prints. I don't go to this bother with all my prints, but with a backlit subject on XP2 film, the selenium treatment on fibre-base Multigrade works wonders, particularly on glazed prints.

No doubt there will be plenty of people wanting to tell me that I could achieve equally good results with far less trouble using resin-coated paper. For the prints in this book, I was asked to print on glossy RC paper. With over 80 negatives, taken over many years, I was very grateful for the short washing time and the easy drying to perfect flatness. And yes, I was perfectly happy with the quality of the prints. My problem with using resin-coated paper for exhibition work, is that I just have not found a satisfactory way of mounting large sheets of this paper – and from what I have seen, I'm not the only one! So for my exhibition prints, I stick with fibre-based paper, mounting them using tissue in a very old dry mounting press (with a recently failed thermostat). This additional hazard in the chain means that I have to watch the thermometer on the press like a hawk to make sure that I only melt the tissue.

Generally, I standardise on a dark grey mount for my exhibition prints, but where the image demands, I occasionally use black or light grey. Recently, I have been mounting on a thin white board with an overlay window mount of a colour to suit the image. The advantage with this system is that the mount colour can be changed to unify a set of pictures or suit an exhibition gallery.

You may have noticed that this brief technical account has concentrated on what happens after the shutter has been pressed. This is because I believe that the actual taking of photographs is, or certainly should be, a personal experience. In any case I am not sure that even I know how I take photographs, beyond setting a shutter speed and adjusting the aperture to line up the needle in my viewfinder. Even these mechanical operations sometimes get forgotten in the panic to focus, frame the scene and press the shutter release before the picture disappears for ever. But then that's candid photography, whether of children or adults. It seems to me to be mostly an intuitive process and thus I am reluctant to analyse it further for fear of becoming self-conscious of the way I work.

The main consideration which I am conscious of is the setting of shutter speed. Working with a hand-held camera, as a tripod is out of the question for most candid work, my main concern is to avoid camera-shake. I usually work at 1/250th of a second, although try to use 1/500 when working with the 200mm lens. I sometimes use a winder, set on single-frame, to allow me to hold the framing while taking several shots.

As to what to photograph, I'm tempted to say that if you don't know, don't bother. But I will not be that negative! The best advice I can offer is to respond: respond to the scenes or situations that excite you visually or emotionally. That way I believe you are likely to produce more interesting images than if you put the technical side of taking a photograph first. The aim has to be to make the technical side second nature so that you can concentrate on the image.

There is one important final point about taking photographs of children, which I hope hardly needs pointing out. It is an absolute rule that the safety and happiness of the child comes first and these must never be jeopardised for the sake of getting a photograph.

To conclude, you will see that there is really nothing unusual about the technical aspects of the way I go about taking child photographs. I think the best advice I can give to anyone wanting to work in this area is to get out there and take lots of photographs – and be as willing to learn from your mistakes as to enjoy your successes.

For a catalogue and further information about other Creative Monochrome publications, please write to:
Creative Monochrome, 20 St Peters Road, Croydon, Surrey, CR0 1HD, England.